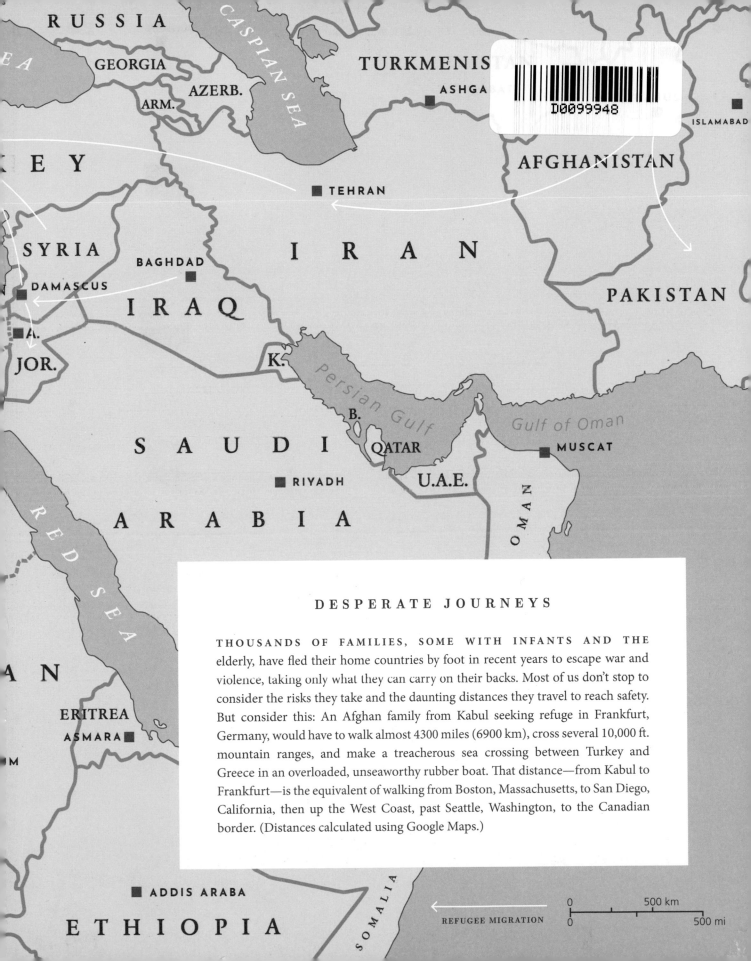

RUSSIA

GEORGIA

AZERB.

ARM.

TURKMENIS

ASHGA

ISLAMABAD

AFGHANISTAN

TEHRAN

KEY

SYRIA

BAGHDAD

IRAN

PAKISTAN

DAMASCUS

IRAQ

A.

JOR.

K.

Persian Gulf

Gulf of Oman

B.

MUSCAT

QATAR

SAUDI

U.A.E.

RIYADH

O M A N

ARABIA

RED SEA

ERITREA

ASMARA

DESPERATE JOURNEYS

THOUSANDS OF FAMILIES, SOME WITH INFANTS AND THE elderly, have fled their home countries by foot in recent years to escape war and violence, taking only what they can carry on their backs. Most of us don't stop to consider the risks they take and the daunting distances they travel to reach safety. But consider this: An Afghan family from Kabul seeking refuge in Frankfurt, Germany, would have to walk almost 4300 miles (6900 km), cross several 10,000 ft. mountain ranges, and make a treacherous sea crossing between Turkey and Greece in an overloaded, unseaworthy rubber boat. That distance—from Kabul to Frankfurt—is the equivalent of walking from Boston, Massachusetts, to San Diego, California, then up the West Coast, past Seattle, Washington, to the Canadian border. (Distances calculated using Google Maps.)

ADDIS ARABA

ETHIOPIA

SOMALIA

REFUGEE MIGRATION

0   500 km

0   500 mi

ADVANCED PRAISE FOR

LET ME TELL YOU MY STORY

"WITH NO POLITICAL POWER, REFUGEES ARE OFTEN LEFT without a voice. *Let Me Tell You My Story* helps refugees reclaim some power and dignity by giving them a platform to tell their stories. It is a meaningful and important collection."

—BRANDON STANTON, AUTHOR OF *HUMANS OF NEW YORK*

"THE POIGNANT STORIES AND COMPELLING IMAGES IN THIS volume provide a powerful counterpoint to the dehumanization of people on the move in Europe and around the world. Highly recommended."

—DR. REECE JONES, AUTHOR OF *VIOLENT BORDERS:
REFUGEES AND THE RIGHT TO MOVE*

"THESE SIMPLE STORIES SPEAK VOLUMES ABOUT THE PLIGHT OF refugees around the world. Through paintings and photographs, full of beauty and dignity, we are privileged to meet real people living the tragedy of refugee life. They are school children, wives and mothers, musicians, journalists, teachers, husbands and fathers. They are African, Asian, Middle Eastern. They are of the world we share. Their loss is palpable, and their courage and yearning to be free shines through on the page. With this book comes hope and a way for readers of all ages to share the emotion and trauma of refugee life and to recognize our shared humanity."

—KAREN LYNN WILLIAMS, COAUTHOR OF *FOUR FEET, TWO SANDALS*
AND PEACE CORP VOLUNTEER (MALAWI)

"PEACE. IT SEEMS SO SIMPLE. BUT SOMEWHERE IN THE WORLD girls get poisoned when they attend school. Some women cannot show their face or they get beaten. Fate determines where and how we live our lives. Together we can better the fate of refugees—people just like us who want to live in freedom. This book is a heartbreaking glimpse into the lives of people who want peace. Let's make sure they don't lose hope."

—MARGRIET RUURS, AUTHOR OF *STEPPING STONES:
A REFUGEE FAMILY'S JOURNEY*

LET ME
TELL YOU
MY STORY

LEAD EDITOR: TWILA BIRD
ASSOCIATE EDITORS: TRISHA LEIMER,
KATHRYN CUNNINGHAM, AND AMY STEVENSON

FAMILIUS

Published by Familius LLC, www.familius.com

Familius books are available at special discounts for bulk purchases, whether for sales promotions or for family or corporate use. For more information, contact Familius Sales at 559-876-2170 or email orders@familius.com.

Reproduction of this book in any manner, in whole or in part, without written permission of the publisher is prohibited.

Some names and identifying details have been changed to protect the privacy and safety of individuals.

Library of Congress Cataloging-in-Publication Data
2018937187
Print ISBN 9781641700498
Ebook ISBN 9781641700948

Printed in China

Edited by Leah Welker

Cover and book design by David Miles

10 9 8 7 6 5 4 3 2

First Edition

LET ME TELL YOU MY STORY

COMPILED BY THEIR STORY IS OUR STORY

REFUGEE
STORIES
OF **HOPE,**
COURAGE,
AND
HUMANITY

TO THOSE FORCED TO
FLEE THEIR
HOMES

AND
TO THOSE
WHO WELCOME
THEM TO NEW ONES.

CONTENTS

ACKNOWLEDGMENTS

THEIR STORY IS OUR STORY (TSOS) GRATEFULLY acknowledges those who believe in our vision of a more welcoming world and offer encouragement and financial support. You know who you are. Thank you.

We're grateful to three award-winning photographers who passionately (and compassionately) dedicate their talents and time in behalf of refugees. Lindsay Silsby (England), Christophe Mortier (France), and Kristi Burton (USA) captured the images we're proud to display in this volume. We're equally appreciative of Utah-based artists Elizabeth Benson Thayer and Nathanael Read, whose powerful paintings, drawings, and etchings help showcase refugee stories. We are honored to have these visual-arts professionals on our team of volunteer humanitarians.

We also thank Lisa Campbell, Greece Project Manager for Do Your Part, an NPO involved in long-term disaster relief. Lisa fearlessly and thoughtfully directed a refugee camp near Athens, Greece, for almost two years. She did not run a charity; she ran a small, self-governing, self-reliant community. Lisa created an oasis of dignity and order by giving camp residents responsibilities and leadership opportunities. She also facilitated our first round of TSOS interviews—our first foray into giving voice to refugees. Thank you, Lisa.

The founders of TSOS in June 2016, on the day they met for the first time in the airport in Frankfurt, Germany. Three of the group flew on to Greece to conduct the first refugee interviews for TSOS. From left to right they are: Trisha Leimer, Germany (president); Elizabeth Thayer, USA (artist); Lindsay Silsby, England (photographer); brothers Garrett and Morgan Gibbons, USA (filmmakers); and Twila Bird, USA (writer). Missing in the photo is Melissa Dalton-Bradford, Germany (writer).

PREFACE

THEIR STORY IS OUR STORY

IN MAY 2016, A PHOTOGRAPHER IN LONDON, A FILMMAKER IN SEATTLE, AND AN artist in Orem, Utah, independently felt the need to put their talents to work for the refugees flooding into Europe. Meanwhile, two humanitarian volunteers in Frankfurt, Germany, were discussing a potential media project designed to share the stories of the displaced people they had been working with. They pulled in a writer in Utah, and through a series of unrelated but incredibly interwoven events, these six individuals came together through social media. Within six weeks they formed Their Story Is Our Story: Giving Voice to Refugees (TSOS).

By July, the TSOS team had raised $10,000, made travel arrangements, and met each other for the first time at the Frankfurt airport to begin a week of filming, photographing, and painting refugees in Greece and Germany. Their plan was to capture fifteen to twenty refugee stories during that week, but to their surprise, they ended up recording over seventy interviews involving nearly two hundred people.

"It was absolutely amazing!" said TSOS president Trisha Leimer. "In the camp in Greece, residents in every tent stood in line to sit down in front of our cameras and talk about their painful, personal experiences. After each interview, they'd stand up, one after the other, take a deep, cleansing breath, then say, 'Thank you. I feel so much better. Thank you for listening.' We hadn't expected that at all."

As Brandon Stanton, the author of *Humans of New York*, discovered— and as the TSOS team learned during their interviews—a basic human need is to be understood, and how better to meet that need than to tell your story? In a February 2018 speech in Salt Lake City, Utah, Brandon explained:

> People share with me things they have never shared with those closest to them. I'm frequently asked, "Brandon, how do you get absolute strangers to admit such personal things in such a short amount of time?" The easy answer to that question is that I just ask. But I think the more complicated answer is that for everybody I talk to there are two threads of thought going through their heads when I explain I'm going to ask them personal questions. One of these threads is, "This conversation is weird, I'm uncomfortable, I don't know this guy." But once they've agreed, they almost never shut me down. They always answer, and I think that's because the other thread is an appreciation for being heard, an appreciation for being listened to. Listening to each other is a scarce commodity. We each need to connect with others and if no one asks, doors remain closed. ("RootsTech General Session 2018: Brandon Stanton," RootsTech.org, accessed April 13, 2018, https://www.rootstech.org/video/general-session-2018-brandon-stanton.)

TSOS is opening doors, opening hearts and opening minds for both those who tell their stories and those who listen. The group is dedicated to helping the refugees tell their own stories in a way that is intimate and emotionally authentic. TSOS also uses photography and art to help shape international dialogue about refugees with the intent to better their situation worldwide.

Since 2016, the TSOS team has expanded to include volunteers from around the world who have stepped forward to help in various ways. TSOS has conducted more interviews, created more artwork, produced short videos for YouTube, and regularly posts new refugee stories on their website, Facebook, Instagram, and Twitter. The team continues to seek new opportunities to promote increased understanding and acceptance of the world's most vulnerable displaced people.

AUTHOR'S NOTE

ALLOWING REFUGEES AND HUMANITARIAN VOLUNTEERS TO tell their own stories is a high priority for TSOS. We videotape interviewees while sitting knee to knee and eye to eye with them, catching every gesture, every facial expression, and every nuance of emotion. After the recorded interviews are professionally translated, TSOS writers work with the translations (or transcriptions in the case of interviews conducted in English) to extract the stories you read here. The editing process, of necessity, leaves fascinating details unwritten in order to fit space requirements for the book. We encourage those who want to know more to visit our website **tsosrefugees.org**, where additional information and photos for each refugee and volunteer are available.

For stories written from a child's point of view, we've used facts expressed by the child's parents to tell the story. Additionally, several stories featuring women are written using information given mostly by their husbands, who were usually the spokespersons for their families.

Many of the people who have shared their stories with us still have family back in their homeland or scattered somewhere along the trail toward freedom who are still in grave danger. Some have powerful enemies and fear retribution even in the places where they currently reside. For this reason we have assigned alias names to many of the subjects of the stories in this book. This also explains why many have asked that we not show their faces. We salute their courage to speak out when so much is at stake, and we ask for your understanding as you open this book and they open their hearts.

The following pages also contain personal expressions from TSOS team members telling what motivates them to donate time, talents, and means to people who are culturally different and sometimes physically distant.

THEIR STORIES

I am still waiting.

I WALKED 3200 MILES SO I CAN
go to school. The borders are closed. It's
been 3 years . . . I am *still* waiting.

———————————————————

HUSNA, AFGHANISTAN

I am separated from my family. I worry about my mother and father every minute.

IN SYRIA, OUR LIVES WERE FULL OF happiness. All our relatives were together, and we were in and out of each other's homes. Our village was quiet even though it was full of people. Not a room was empty.

ISIS invaded our village on the first day of the revolution. They began killing people without mercy because we don't share their religion. They forced a religion on us, calling it an Islamic state. They kept killing—they killed so many. They didn't bury them; they threw them in pits. Now Syria is under siege and our whole lives are destroyed.

Anyone who smokes gets their hand cut off. If they see a woman's face, they hit her. They take whoever is going or coming. They accuse you of something, anything, and then they take you away, and before you know it, your body has been beaten up from how much they hit you. They take fourteen-and fifteen-year-olds and drag them into the army.

For my safety, my father sent me with my aunt to travel to Germany. It took us three months to get here. I am separated from my family. I worry about my mother and father every minute. If my family isn't around me, I think about them all the time. Now the borders are closed. They can't come here, and I can't go there. Every time I talk to my family, I cry and fall apart before I finish talking. My father loves me. I was happy in Syria.

FIROZ, SYRIA

Wc had to go
into hiding.

OUR FUTURE IS NOT IN OUR
hands. My husband's car business
did well until the Taliban demanded
that he traffic weapons for them. He
refused. We had to go into hiding,
and finally we were forced to leave.

HAKIMA, AFGHANISTAN

KELLIE JOLLEY, USA

TSOS public relations coordinator

ONE OF THE BRIGHTEST LIGHTS TO illuminate my life came in the form of a young refugee and a simple opportunity. My introduction to him was preceded by personal tragedy.

In early 2015, life dramatically changed for my family when my husband was diagnosed with stage-four brain cancer; the doctors gave him three months to live. Although our family spent every valuable minute together, his loss was enormous and took a deep toll on all of us. The following months were trying and emotionally heavy.

One night I was looking through Facebook and a video story from Italy came up on my feed. I started to watch the unbelievable story of Bolaji Adepoju, a Nigerian refugee whose two brothers were drowned while trying to reach Italy on an overloaded, unseaworthy boat. Miraculously, Bolaji survived. After his rescue, he made a solemn promise to God that he would serve Him by teaching people that God knows them and loves them.

As I watched his story of heartbreak and loss, I felt an instant connection to him. The part of me that was grieving for our own family tragedy needed to be filled. I knew I had to do more than just listen to his story. I wanted to help and comfort him. What could I do? How could I help?

After a little digging, I sent a message to the man who posted Bolaji's story; he served as Bolaji's church leader in Rome. I told him who I was and how deeply I desired to help this young man in any way I could. He connected us, and since that first introduction, Bolaji and I have been writing each other every week for the past two years without fail. The connection he shares with my kids and me is one that has ascended to the level of family. Through shared stories and pictures, testimonies of faith and growth, and a constant stream of love, Bolaji has become someone we adore and rely on for light, joy, and inspiration.

TRISHA LEIMER, GERMANY

TSOS president

IN 2015, WORLD EVENTS BROUGHT A flood of people from countries like Afghanistan, Syria, Eritrea, and Nigeria into Germany, where I had been living with my family for over fifteen years. Despite our very different cultures and traditions, and although we don't share the same religion or language, we have discovered much more that connects than divides us. We have the same basic needs, wants, hopes, and fears. And as we have carefully and respectfully reached across the few barriers that do exist and shared of ourselves, our original fears and hesitancies have turned into mutual understanding and respect. What the world has called a "crisis" has changed me forever. I have become a better person.

MELISSA DALTON-BRADFORD, GERMANY

TSOS writer and speaker

AS A BEREAVED MOTHER (WE LOST OUR firstborn eighteen-year-old son to a tragic drowning), and as a mother who has raised her family over twenty international moves, I am sensitized to others' losses and invested in their survival. I bond to them on my broken edges.

And who among these refugees has not been broken? Lost a home, a language, a culture, a beloved? Or many beloveds? Or all their beloveds? I lost my beloved in a world of peace and plenty, not to the senselessness of a suicide bomb, Taliban torture, a sniper shot, or any act of extremism. Am I somehow deserving of all my blessings and privileges and refugees are deserving of their desperation? Of course not. I have been given so much—peace, prosperity, health, freedom, and more—not as some sort of reward but as a sacred responsibility.

FOR INFORMATION ON
HOW *YOU* CAN HELP, SEE
PAGE 228.

CARTER CHARLES, FRANCE

TSOS translation coordinator

I WAS BARELY THREE YEARS OLD WHEN my father fled Haiti's Duvalier regime and emigrated to the United States; he didn't speak a word of English. After his rescue in American waters by the US Coast Guard, they took him to Florida, his dream destination, instead of returning him to Haiti. I reunited with him thirty-six years later, a few months before his passing. He was still torn inside because of the loved ones (including me) he had had to leave behind.

When I was ten, my mother emigrated to French Guiana, where she lived in hiding and in constant fear of deportation. I followed the same path when I was fifteen, traveling under a false identity through Curaçao and Suriname, and crossing the Maroni River that connects the two countries in an unregistered canoe. I recovered my real identity and studied in French Guiana, then later in mainland France and in the United States, earning a PhD in American studies with an emphasis in sociology and history of religions.

Today I am happy to pay back whatever France has invested in the illegal immigrant that I was; I teach hundreds of students English as a second language in addition to business English, translation, and American Studies. I've also assisted refugees and immigrants in France with translations and paperwork.

Sometimes the Taliban would tear
away your skin while you are alive
because you are Shia.

WE LIVED IN A VALLEY NEAR KABUL THAT was controlled by the Taliban. ISIS was there, too. We were told we would be beheaded if we disobeyed orders to raise their flags in our village. As Shia, we were not secure; we had continuous threats. I was tortured three times. Sometimes the Taliban would tear away your skin while you are alive because you are Shia.

We decided to leave and sold everything we had; there is no way back. The regional leader will arrest us and will definitely behead us if we return.

I am responsible for my own family—my wife and four children—but also for my sister and nephew, who are both deaf and mute. I am a man, and I am stuck in this way.

ILHAN, AFGHANISTAN

I'VE BEEN DEAF AND MUTE SINCE BIRTH.
When I was old enough, I was forced to marry the
head of our region. My parents were too old to protest;
they ran away, and we have heard no news about them.
I escaped with my brother, and now we are in Europe.
I only want to live in a country that is peaceful and
[where] there is no threat.

RADWA, AFGHANISTAN

Based on interview with Radwa's brother.

I am lost.

I CAME FROM WEST AFRICA BECAUSE
of a political problem; my uncle was impeached,
our home was vandalized, and all of my family
ran away. Our leaders are just leading the
economy of the country and not leading the
people. I did not wish to leave my country, but
we have war in Africa.

One of my friends took me on the Libya
route. I stayed in Libya for one month in a prison
with two of my friends. One died in the prison—
my friend who rescued me. They are shooting
and killing people there. Later, they took me to
do farm work, and from there I ran away and
paid my way to go to the seaside, where I met
people going on a ship, and I crossed to Italy.

I have been here in Italy one year and six
months. It's not easy for me. I am lost. I've not
seen my family, my friends, or people from my
childhood. I can't shape my life to this different
society; I'm not used to it. I'm feeling bad. The
people reject me, and I need a lawyer for my
documents. My stress is growing. I'm not talking
or doing anything. I'm just in the town sleeping
and eating. I used to have a job working to make
mechanical generators. I want to work. Human
beings are supposed to work. Work for myself
and the generation after me. I want to leave
something for my children and grandchildren.
The Italians give me a place to sleep and food,
but I need help finding a job. If a person doesn't
know English or Italian, he cannot get a job.

If I leave the camp for more than three
days, they will not let me back. They put me on
the streets begging for my daily bread. Italians,
according to what I see, do not easily like us
because of differences. Maybe what they know I
don't know, and what I know they don't know.
They are white; I am black; but we are all human.

TAMBA, WEST AFRICA

30

Even though our journey was so hard, I
brought my Koran and my prayer rug with me.
I carried them on my back.

WE LEFT IRAN BECAUSE WE ARE AFGHANS. WE weren't allowed to work, so we couldn't pay the rent. And we have enemies in Iran. My daughter has nightmares. She's still afraid because of what happened to her, what they did to her.

We sold everything in Iran. We suffered while we were going through the mountains in Turkey. Sometimes I crawled on my hands and knees. We had to throw away all of our clothes, anything that was too heavy. It was so hard; we lost hope. We thought we were going to die. Then it was really hard coming down. It took thirteen or fourteen hours, and I could barely walk. At the end, I fell in a hole in the mountain that was full of water.

Even though our journey was so hard, I brought my Koran and my prayer rug with me. I carried them on my back. I love my religion.

I remember one part of our journey was in the sea and I was afraid we would drown. I asked God to help us. All of a sudden, the sea got really peaceful. He helped us. Whenever I felt I couldn't continue anymore, I asked God and He helped us. Now, even though my knee doesn't work and it hurts very much, I make sure to say my prayers every day. When I can't sleep at night I pray most of all for my children who are still in Afghanistan and Iran. I get so afraid that our enemies will find them and hurt them.

Here in Germany, we have new friends who bring us clothes. It makes me happy to have true friends who are so good and kind. In the refugee camp, we sleep in beds, which is better than sleeping wet beside the shore in the cold. The Germans are so nice. For the rest of my life, I will serve them because they help us. I hope the government will let me stay here and that my children can go to school to get an education. This is all of my life.

RASHEEDA, AFGHANISTAN

MY MIDDLE SON LOST
his life to the bomb. My oldest
lost his mind.

YOSUF, AFGHANISTAN

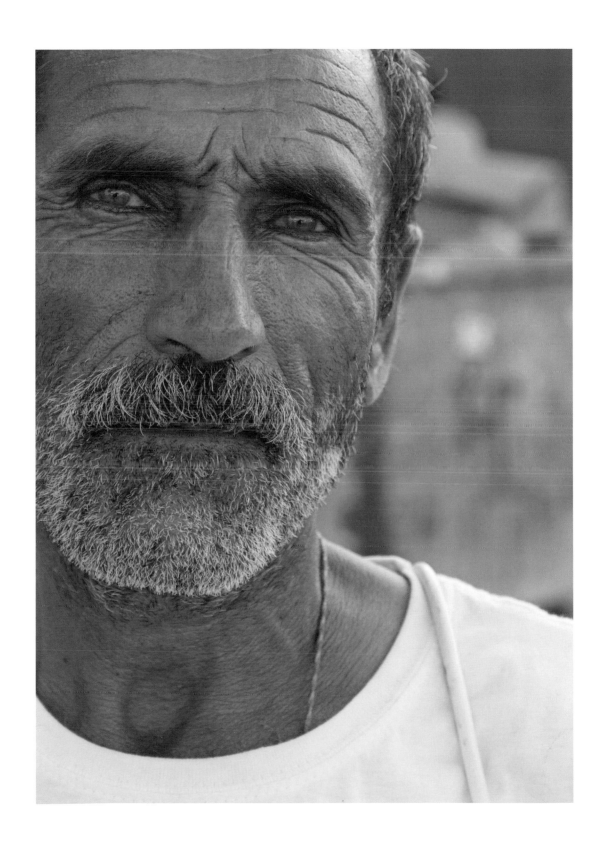

DIANA LEVATON, FRANCE

IN SEPTEMBER 2015, WE WERE SITTING in our Paris living room watching the national news, just like any other family, and we watched footage of countless refugees walking across Europe. It deeply touched me. More particularly, it touched my son, Ben, who had just turned fifteen. In the following days, we discussed his grandfather, my husband's father, who had walked along that same path as a Ukranian Jew fleeing from the Russian pogroms in 1920. With his family, he was basically running for his life. He walked all the way to Paris and ended up sleeping on the same streets where today's refugees are now.

That was the spark which led us to form the group Compassion Without Borders. I organized parents; Ben organized students and faculty. At first we exported supplies to Germany because that was initially where the focus was, but then we heard whispers about refugees right here in our own city, so we went out looking for them.

I will never forget the sensation of walking out of the Stalingrad Metro Station and tripping over a body. That body was one of four thousand in a sea of sleeping bags and tents. People with nothing. People shivering in T-shirts. It was the most shocking thing I've ever seen in my life. It was unimaginable right here in Paris!

At that point, we shifted our focus to the people right under our noses. We began connecting with other volunteers. With the help of hundreds of others who were determined to keep these people alive, we were able to gather and distribute huge amounts of food on an ongoing basis. Ben was passionate about it, and I was willing to walk through fire to help him stay involved.

I think there's something about being on the right side of history. Some day people will look back at this time and ask, "What did you do to help during the refugee crisis?" I want Ben to be able to respond with the satisfaction of knowing he did the right thing.

BEN LEVATON, FRANCE

WHEN OUR STUDENT GROUP, Compassion Without Borders, first began serving the refugees on a personal, one-on-one basis, we were hesitant and a little bit afraid. But we got over that and were able to really make a difference. We handed out sandwiches and personal supplies. I felt good about what we were doing, and I know the others felt that way, too.

Refugee support eventually grew beyond our school community. Other individuals and organizations in Paris soon helped in the humanitarian effort. Even the famous French cooking school, Le Cordon Bleu, found a way to help. They donated hundreds of cakes produced by student chefs (which normally get thrown away) to Compassion Without Borders. Sales of Le Cordon Bleu's throw-away cakes raised thousands of dollars to help purchase supplies for refugees.

There are opportunities to help refugees all around the world right now. One person can make a difference. One person begins, then others join in and assist. Our effort started from nothing—just look what has happened! We've been able to help thousands of refugees living here.

CHRISTINE DOLAN, FRANCE

MY NAME IS CHRISTINE DOLAN. I AM from Yorkshire, England, and I've lived in France for thirty years. One day I was out and decided I'd take a left instead of a right, and to my shock and horror I saw hundreds and hundreds of refugees sleeping in tents—here, in Paris! I hung around to see who was in charge, began chatting, and decided to come back later with a bag of cuddly toys I'd been hanging on to. That's how I started, just over two years ago.

When I trek to where refugees are camped, what I always do first is try to find someone who speaks English who can be my translator; that makes things a hundred times easier. I worked with a nurse for a while because so many of the people were sick, especially the babies. At one point I got involved in distributing socks. People sent me socks from all over the world. I was called the Sock Ambassador.

There are many desperate people—lots of trauma, suicides, illness, and depression. Initially, I did not want to get involved in listening to peoples' individual stories because it's so heartbreaking. It can be overwhelming for volunteers; we have to fight cracking emotionally. I've seen about 100,000 people in these last two years, and I want to help each one, but I can't. I keep helping, anyway.

MATTHEW LONGHURST, USA

TSOS treasurer, board member

I AM THE PRODUCT NOT JUST OF immigrants but also of refugees. Whether their persecutions were religious, economic, social, or natural, many of my ancestors were uprooted in fear and turmoil. For me, the refugee crisis of the last several years has closely coincided with a growing knowledge of and a strong sense of connection to my forebears. My ancestors' life experiences echo the stories of so many whose stories TSOS has shared over the last two years. Today's refugees must combat suspicion, distrust, and even xenophobia and racism in heavy doses. I cannot help but feel a deep obligation to help where I can.

FOR INFORMATION ON
HOW *YOU* CAN HELP, SEE
PAGE 228.

I LEFT MY COUNTRY BECAUSE I LOST SOMEONE VERY CLOSE to me and I lost my job. I was having a psychological problem. My friend told me he had some money and that I should go follow a troop of boys to Libya.

Libya, it was hell. To cross the desert, we were about twenty-four in the truck. Some Arabs on motorcycles jumped us in the middle of the night and started shooting. Eight of our people died. For about two days we were in the desert. We had no place to hide. We were drinking our own urine. Only six of us came out alive.

We were able to move to a transit camp called Duruku. We lost more people in the desert, but six of us made it through there to Sabha, Libya. There was more shooting there in the middle of the night. A whole family was kidnapped, but they left us. Most of us had injuries.

When I got to Tripoli, I was able to find a temporary job at an Egyptian bakery, but then I had problems. Libyan soldiers occasionally came and picked us up to take to their barracks. They asked me to squat, cover my ears, and jump up and down. They forced me down and took my clothes off. One of them wanted to rape me in the hall where they keep ammunition. I shouted, and one of his colleagues came and asked him to stop.

I talked to some other boys from my country; we decided to cross the sea to Italy. When I saw the sea, I didn't want to go. I could swim only a little. My friends encouraged me and said they would cover my eyes. I thought I would die. I said, "God, OK, if today is my last day, let it be."

I have been here in Italy two months. I am calming down. I have confidence that if I go to bed nobody will break the door and if I am sick I will get medicine. I move freely and feel secure. My thinking is no longer harsh or negative.

IDEHEN, WEST AFRICA

Libya, it was hell.

If you have a child, you will understand how I feel.

MY NAME IS GHEZAL. I AM THIRTY-FIVE years old, and I have seven children. I am from a village near the city of Herat, where there is war most of the time. The Taliban says we are all infidels. They killed my father, one of my sisters, and a brother. My husband was killed two years ago. One day, he went to the market to shop, and on the way back to the house he was killed. I didn't see his body. I just saw one photo of his death.

After that, I lived with my brother, and he supported us. But he worked for the government, and because of this, the Taliban threatened to kill him, so he left Afghanistan and moved to Germany. I thought we should leave as well. My son-in-law sold his house to provide money for our journey. In the end, I had to leave my three oldest daughters behind. They are thirteen, fifteen, and sixteen years old.

We only had enough money to go from Afghanistan to Turkey and from Turkey to Greece. I had terrible times on our long journey with my little children. Sometimes we had nothing to eat for two or three days. Some nights I stayed awake until morning because I was afraid wolves or thieves would attack us in the forest.

Now we are in Greece, but my heart and my mind are still in Afghanistan with my daughters. If you have a child, you will understand how I feel. It has been one year since I came here, and they are there and they need help. One daughter is married, and two are living with my mother in our village. It is very dangerous there, even worse than Kabul. There isn't any phone or internet connection in the village to contact them. I am afraid my husband's family will sell my daughters to the Taliban. I'm crying every night here, and only God knows what I'm feeling.

Ghezal's worst fears were confirmed when the Taliban gruesomely murdered her thirteen-year-old daughter in Afghanistan in March 2017.

GHEZAL, AFGHANISTAN

If I have to try forty more times, I will not stop until I get out of Greece.

I AM A JOURNALIST. I LIVED IN KABUL. I WROTE SOME reports about the Taliban for the media, and they sent me a threatening letter, but I did not care. I continued my job. But then the Taliban bombed one of the television stations and sent a letter to all journalists threatening their lives.

After this, my family—my mother and my sister—were worried for me. We didn't have a lot of money, but they decided I should take all we had and go. It costs about 10,000 euros to pay a smuggler to get from Turkey to Germany. They [my family] said they would come later. So I came alone. But they are not safe. I hope to go to Germany where I can begin to earn money to send for them.

For two months I was in Moria [a refugee camp on the Island of Lesbos]. Every night there were fights. Moria is not safe. But I came without papers, and they wouldn't let me go. It was like a jail. There was a fence, but I noticed a place where it was breaking, so I got through it and ran up onto the hillside. I saw the police were coming after me, so I began to run. I can run very fast. I was on the national running team for Afghanistan. I got away. I ran to the port and jumped on a ship that was just pulling away.

Now I'm here on the mainland of Greece, but I can't stay here. There are so many people who have lost everything, and there is no work for any of us.

I've already tried ten times to cross the border into Macedonia or Bulgaria, but each time I've been caught by the Greek police, the Serbian police, or the Bulgarian police . . . If I have to try forty more times, I will not stop until I get out of Greece.

About a month after Bilal's interview, he went swimming with friends in the ocean, got caught in a riptide, and drowned. He was twenty-three years old.

BILAL, AFGHANISTAN

AT EIGHTEEN, FATE PLACED ALI AND HIS FAMILY *in the center of hostilities in northern Afghanistan. Warring militant factions killed hundreds of people in his village. Ali helped identify and bury dozens of his friends and neighbors in a mass grave.*

Though he walked on an old, second-hand prosthetic leg after losing his left leg in an explosion a few years earlier, Ali decided to undertake the long journey out of his country to save his life. He joined a group of families who were also fleeing the violence. Two of the mothers were traveling without their husbands who had gone ahead to find places to stay. Along the way, Ali encouraged and protected them, and sometimes carried their children. They traveled together by bus, on foot, and in smugglers' cars.

We spent days and nights in the mountains and blocked on the borders. I crossed the mountainous border between Afghanistan and Pakistan walking with my handicap. Then it took us another sixteen hours to cross the border between Pakistan and Iran, also in very high mountains of more than 2500 meters. The Iranian police were killing people on the borders. We saw people in the mountains who were dead—some from hunger, some were shot.

The rough terrain caused Ali's plastic leg to break several times. He repaired it with sticks and duct tape but by the time he reached Greece—a journey of 4,900 km (3,045 miles)—he was in great pain.

Ali made it to Greece just as the Balkan route closed, which blocked his progress to central Europe. He stayed in two refugee camps—one on the island of Lesbos, the second near Athens where he quickly formed friendships with other residents and volunteers, chief among them Bilal, another Afghan refugee. Bilal accompanied Ali to Athens the day he was fitted with a new, state-of-the-art prosthetic leg, which was purchased by a generous donor.

I was happy in this camp. I almost forgot how hard life can be until the day I lost my best friend. Bilal's English was very good. He was working with volunteers in the camp's school. One day he left to teach English. He told me he planned to swim to an island afterwards. I don't know what happened. He lost his life. Bilal died in the water. After that, I left Greece. I couldn't stay.

I kept thinking, "I will be dead;
I'm not going to make it!

*"Here's a picture of me and four others in the trunk of a Peugeot.
This is how we crossed the Iranian territory. In total, this smuggler's
car transported seventeen people. We each paid 600 Euros."*

But the European borders were closed. Bulgaria was closed. Everything from Greece was closed. I hid under a truck [a semitrailer truck] when the driver was off his shift. I lay underneath on top of a cross beam and waited for five or six hours before he came back. He didn't see me. Then the truck began moving. I lay under it for thirty-six hours—no food, little water. It was very, very dangerous. I kept thinking, "I will be dead; I'm not going to make it!"

I spent fifteen days in Italy then went to France with a smuggler. When I arrived in Paris, I felt completely lost. I asked a Frenchman how to get to Jaures Metro Station. (I heard that this was where the refugees were.) When I arrived there, I was completely shocked. I saw more than 3,000 refugees who slept and lived under the bridges, on the streets, whereever they could basically. . . . Because of my leg, I was a lot more vulnerable; it was very difficult for me to sleep under the bridge, especially because it was very cold. My artificial limb broke down and injured my leg.

Knowing his new prosthetic, which he had used briefly in Greece was worth over ten thousand dollars, Ali had left it behind rather than risk having it stolen and sold by smugglers. He wore his old one during the months he lived on the streets in Paris among the other refugees. He had only a thin jacket to keep him warm in the soggy, winter weather.

Eventually, volunteers found him a safe place to stay and arranged for his new prosthetic to be transported from Greece. Currently, Ali has an apartment, speaks French, and reaches out to his fellow displaced countrymen.

ALI, AFGHANISTAN

THERE'S MORE TO THE STORY:
HTTPS://TSOSREFUGEES.ORG/BOOK/LINKS/2

I didn't let them go to school when we were in Kabul because I was afraid the Taliban would kidnap them.

WE LEFT OUR COUNTRY BECAUSE the Taliban tried to kill my husband several times. We were seeking a better place, and now we are helpless refugees. We never imagined we would have to live in a tent.

We are in a very bad situation now. We are exhausted, and we can't go back to our country where my husband's life was threatened. We hope this awful situation will be over soon and our children can go to school after having missed two years. I didn't let them go to school when we were in Kabul because I was afraid the Taliban would kidnap them in order to find their father. Now my children have no destiny.

ZAKEELA, AFGHANISTAN

I want to have my own family,
my own home.

MY NAME IS LAYLA. I'M FROM ETHIOPIA. I LEFT ALMOST ten years ago. At that time, I was very young, maybe twenty years old. There was no opportunity to work, and I thought maybe I could have a better life. So I left my country and went to Syria to work for three years. After that, I went to Turkey by boat, then to Greece for five years. My daughter was born there. Then I came to Germany. I walked. I carried my daughter on my back for days and days.

First we lived in a room with four people. One was an old woman from Somalia, and sometimes she beat my baby if she was noisy. Then I lived in a very small hotel. There was no place for my daughter to play. When we wanted to eat, we didn't have any place to cook. The mattress, it was so dirty! I had an allergic reaction, but they didn't want to change the mattress. I couldn't sleep in that place anymore, so they transferred me to another place.

They took me to a gym. I had my daughter with me, and I was pregnant again. We didn't have a room. Men, women, everybody slept together. Imagine! I couldn't sleep. More than anything, I was afraid. Not for me. For me, no problem. I had suffered a lot before coming to this place. I was afraid something would happen to my daughter. All the time I was crying, crying, crying.

Now I am here in the Women's Shelter with my two children. The father of my baby is not here. He is living in London. What I wish for the most is to have my family, like before. Almost ten years ago I lived in a family. I had my father, I had my brothers—everything. I want to have my own family, my own home. I want to know this is my place. I want to be able to say, "This is *my* house. We can stay forever here and nobody will tell me to go."

LAYLA, ETHIOPIA

FATIMA DZHAFAROVA, FRANCE

FATIMA WAS BORN IN MOSCOW, LIVED *in Dubai for five years, and is now a student at the American School of Paris. After attending a school assembly in 2016 which featured Melissa Dalton-Bradford, an international author and humanitarian who spoke eloquently in behalf of the thousands of refugees who were streaming into Europe, she was hooked.*

It was one of the strongest presentations we've ever had. No one said a word after Melissa was through speaking. It was dead silence—very strange in a high school. I decided then and there I wanted to become involved in helping refugees. I joined the school's newly formed club, Compassion Without Borders.

Once our Compassion Without Borders group sponsored a bus tour of Paris for refugee teenagers. We each prepared a presentation for a specific site in Paris. Mine was on the Eiffel Tower. The bus was full. The refugee teens looked so different from us, but they were happy, excited, and eager for the tour. That changed my perspective about them. I guess I expected them to be sad and depressed, but they were so light-hearted. That was cool.

In addition to stopping at various sites, we played games, chatted, and took selfies—really cool ones because they all had selfie sticks. We were interspersed on the bus so we each had refugees to talk to. Their English was limited, so we didn't have deep conversations, but we all laughed together and had a good time.

JULIE ANDERSON, GERMANY

I WANTED TO HELP REFUGEES IN A personal way after they began flooding into Germany, where I live with my family. I established a library in an unused restaurant located near the Rebstock refugee camp in Frankfurt. Combining donated books with those I purchased after setting up a Go Fund Me campaign, we soon had over thirteen hundred books to stock the refugee lending library. I cataloged them as in a normal library.

Others found out about the library. Soon volunteers came in to play games with the children. Some helped tutor them with their schoolwork on Tuesdays and Thursdays. Everyone has something they can give. Figuring that out and being willing to do it, even though it's scary and outside of your comfort zone, is important.

Refugees can come into regular German public libraries but can't check out books until they have permanent addresses and begin paying taxes. And there's a stigma; it's difficult for them to go into a cultural institution they're not familiar with when they don't speak the language. That's part of why I thought the refugee library was good, too, because it provided an intermediary experience. Refugees can learn how to use a library in a comfortable place.

I'll never forget the women's joy when we got a copy of the Koran in German! That's a sacred book to them, and for them to look up familiar verses and learn them in German was a great example of how God cares about the details of our lives.

LYDIA DEFRANCHI NELSON, USA

PERHAPS THE LIFELONG PRIVILEGE I'VE enjoyed is why the stories of refugees torn from their homes struck me so hard. It is difficult to fathom the unfairness of a life interrupted. And the indifference of governments and nations is discouraging.

What is it like to be someone raging at an impenetrable wall?

MEGAN CARSON, USA

TSOS social media coordinator

WHEN I FIRST READ AND WATCHED THE stories of families crowding into boats, fleeing for safety, and seeking refuge, I was horrified at and my heart ached for the combination of terror, loss, and pain they undoubtedly experienced. My heart ached when I heard disparaging comments from others,

which reflected fear and misunderstanding about who these refugees really were.

Not living anywhere near the crisis, I felt helpless but yearned to do something—anything. Though it seemed small and insignificant, I started selling my homemade bread to raise money to donate to refugees. It gave me something to do, while also bringing awareness to refugees, at least among my circle of family and friends. Then I connected with people and organizations that provided help to refugees in other ways.

My hope is that we can find unity in our mutual sorrow and healing through our common humanity.

MARGO WATSON, USA

TSOS donor and media relations coordinator

I TOO HAVE FACED TRAGEDY WITH THE sudden deaths of a fiancé and of a husband, but I hope my children have learned from the Gethsemanes I've faced that we can't always choose what happens to us, but we can choose how we respond. We can overcome, be our best selves, and help others along the way.

FOR INFORMATION ON
HOW *YOU* CAN HELP, SEE
PAGE 228.

AFTER I FINISHED SCHOOL, I STARTED TRAVELING to try to find better jobs. I worked in Nigeria, Ghana, and the Ivory Coast, then someone asked me to come to Libya to work. That's when I discovered that Libya is a dead zone.

When we got there, military gangs searched us for everything we had. They took it all. They don't work; they just want to get money or other things. If you are a girl along the roadside, they will want you to sleep with them or [give them something], or you won't be able to pass.

Fifteen-year-old boys had guns, and they drove good cars. If you touched them, or looked at them, or said something they didn't like, they would shoot you. The humans there are like animals.

It was interesting for me seeing this strange life. It was like I was in a movie. But at the end of the day, it wasn't playful. I worried about how my life would end. . . .

One time the street boys broke into our house, took what they wanted, and tried to take our money. (We had to hide our money in our shoes or inside the waistbands of our jeans.) I was asleep and woke up to find that the boy next to me was shot dead. I decided then I needed to go somewhere else.

Now I am in Rome. My life hasn't gone as I wished, but it is meant to be. It's God's plan. I'm twenty-five. Five years from now, if I'm blessed, I'll have all my documents in order, get married, and have a good job.

Everyone has his own road and his own destiny. So I choose my own road to follow, and I'm grateful for the destiny God has for me. My dream is to help people make life better. I don't want to see others pass through what I've passed through or see what I have seen. I believe it's not what you acquire in your own life but what you invest in the lives of others that is most important.

RHENALD, NIGERIA

THERE'S MORE TO THE STORY:
HTTPS://TSOSREFUGEES.ORG/BOOK/LINKS/10

TEARS ARE RUNNING IN MY EYES BECAUSE when I was in my country, I had my family—my wife and two children. I was taking good care of them. I had a job.

I lived in a West African country, where I was president of an okada [motorcycle taxi] organization. We employed thousands of youth. Then the government, they said they don't want okadas in the capital city. But this is how the youth sustained their life. They used the money to take care of their families. It's how I sustained my family.

There was a riot. Police in the streets started shooting live bullets and tear gas. After two days the newspapers said they wanted the president and executive members of the Bikeriders' Union dead or alive. I didn't have an option. I took my wife and two children to Niger.

I decided to go to Libya to look for a job. I had been there in 2004, and it was good when Gaddafi was president. My wife said, "You go ahead, and when you have a job and a place to stay, I can join you." I didn't want to leave her with both of our children to take care of, so my daughter came with me.

We went to Libya. We were in the desert for six days with only water to drink. My daughter was only seven. When we reached Libya, rebel Arab people caught us. They took everything. Then I didn't have my phone to communicate with my wife. We were forced into a boat and they took us to Italy.

My wife tried to find me in Libya. Someone told me my wife was in prison [there] and if I gave them money, they would release her. I sent it for my wife, and they released her, but I didn't want her to go through Libya again. I told her to return to our home. So now my wife and son are there, and my daughter and I are in Italy. But I praise God that my family is safe.

MICHAEL, WESTERN AFRICA

We went to Libya. We were in the desert for six days with only water to drink. My daughter was only seven.

I LOVE MUSIC! I LOVE PLAYING THE GUITAR, and I love to sing. My goal has always been music. Even as a child, I sang all the time growing up. My family couldn't understand it. They said, "What are you doing with all that singing? You are driving us crazy!" After serving the required two years in the Iranian military, I returned to my city and secretly began learning to play the guitar. I joined a band and ended up getting in trouble with the Islamic police for playing music that wasn't allowed by the government. I had to go. It was not at all easy to leave Iran. I didn't have any money. Finally, I sold my motorcycle and borrowed some money from my relatives. I left.

In Germany I have been able to achieve more than I was ever allowed to in Iran. What I didn't receive in Iran, I have received here—love and respect. In Iran it is very difficult to find a friend you can trust. I am now in Germany. I am learning the German language. I began attending a music school. I am allowed to play for friends and to sing. I know that I can follow my dream to make music. And I know that I can achieve that goal here. I can now become what I always wanted to be, a musician.

PARSA, IRAN

I joined a band and ended up
getting in trouble with the Islamic
police for playing music that wasn't
allowed by the government.

Their childhood is lost. I have
missed three years of their lives.
I will never get them back.

OUR HOME IN ALEPPO WAS BOMBED.

We fled to Turkey all together—my four sons, my husband, and I—but we only had enough money to pay the smuggler for two of us to get to Europe. My husband told me to go to Germany with our youngest son because I am a math teacher and can speak English, and because I am strong.

After two years of being separated and trying very hard to bring them to me, my husband became sick. He has been diagnosed with Crohn's disease. That was one year ago, and no matter how hard I try, we are being kept apart. I feel so helpless. I don't feel strong anymore. I can't sleep, I get dizzy, and there is a constant ringing in my ears. Some days I can't even get out of bed.

I worry about my three teenage sons, who not only don't have their mother but must now take care of their father and worry about how to eat and pay for his medicine. Their childhood is lost. I have missed three years of their lives. I will never get them back.

KAMARIA, SYRIA

I must be strong for her.

I LIKE BEING IN SCHOOL AGAIN. My teacher says my German is really good. My mother asks me to make the phone calls and brings me to important appointments to translate. I must be strong for her. She worries a lot and gets tired. While she sleeps, I play games on her cell phone.

ARIF, SYRIA

ELIZABETH THAYER:

Their whole lives were destroyed: comfortable homes, communities, families, studies, steady jobs, and hopes for the future. They fled, carrying little but the hope of a safer future with them. Now they wait, paused for who knows how long in tents on the site of an abandoned factory in Greece. Comparatively speaking, it is not the worst place to wait. This camp has the luxuries of a small schoolroom, a medical unit, an electric strip for charging phones, two rows of porta potties, and a shower unit . . . and running water from a hose for drinking and for washing. For most, running water used to be a common convenience that was taken for granted. Now, like the hope that keeps them going day in and day out, it is a precious, sustaining necessity.

Barbara Kingsolver wrote, "The very least you can do in your life is figure out what you hope for. And the most you can do is live inside that hope. Not admire it from a distance but live right in it, under its roof." And that is what these refugees do. They cling to hope in an ocean of uncertainty. In the words of Hamed, a refugee in the camp, "Other than hope, we don't have anything else. Every day the refugees keep praying and nobody hears their voice except God. They are still waiting. But still, we have hope."

RUNNING WATER

Oil on linen, TSOS artist Elizabeth Benson Thayer

You know girls have no value here.

WE ARE FOUR SISTERS; MY OLDER SISTER IS married, the rest of us are not. After our father died, we had no one to protect us. Our uncles wanted to forcibly marry the rest of us off. They told my mother, "Your girls must marry anybody we tell them to. Daughters have no right to protest, and they should not talk back at all. You know girls have no value here."

Our mother quarreled with my uncles and remained awake each night to protect us from the danger posed by someone coming to our house in secret and carrying us off. We lived in insecurity.

My brother-in-law defended us, and they threatened to kill him. He lost everything to help us escape. So we left.

We faced many hardships to get here. Now we have enough security to sleep safely.

Sharoreh and her sisters are safe, but their dreams of continuing their education are fading as they languish in refugee camps, first in Greece and now in Serbia. They need a place to call home.

SHAROREH AND HER BROTHER, DAVOD, AFGHANISTAN

DURING THE SYRIAN CIVIL WAR IN 2014, *Aeham Ahmad became a YouTube presence by playing an old upright piano in the bombed-out ruins of Yarmouk, a suburb of Damascus, Syria. Fame wasn't his goal. All he wanted was to bring a little happiness into the lives of his neighbors, to keep everyone from losing their minds. Aeham, a classically trained pianist, and his friends would roll the piano around the streets on a rusty green vegetable cart. Wherever they stopped, families looking for relief from the endless fighting would join them. Children would sing along, and their parents would nod to their music.*

"I wanted to give them a beautiful dream. I wanted to change this black color at least into gray.

Music makes us happy, full of energy, and full of lovely things in the heart, but it doesn't make anything for the stomach. In Yarmouk, I couldn't make falafels for 100,000 people, but I could play music for 100,000 people. When the children saw the piano, I played, and it made them happy. There was only a small place for happiness because it was mostly sadness, a lot of dying there. And it was very dangerous in the street. A sniper killed Zana when she was playing the piano beside me. Yes, he shot her in the head. She was only twelve.

Videos of Aeham's street performances spread online, first among Syrians, then more widely to the rest of the world. He became a symbol of hope and defiance, showing there were human beings with real lives stuck in Yarmouk. But his notoriety also brought condemnation from ISIS, which banned western music. So they torched his piano.

That was the breaking point for Aeham. He left and made his way to Europe. His first boat from Turkey to Greece sank, and several people drowned. Already widely known for his piano videos, he filmed his second crossing for the BBC. Once he was safely in Europe, he started posting his progress on Facebook. Everywhere he went, he found people who knew the story of the "Piano Man of Yarmouk." He was received with open arms when he arrived in Germany. His message of resilience made him Germany's most popular

Oil on linen, TSOS artist Elizabeth Benson Thayer

I had good memories with my music before, but now I play music with a lot of pain because I have pain. They clap for me, but those back in Syria are still in prison, under siege, under bombs.

refugee. Soon, he was booked for piano performances almost every night, crisscrossing the country from modest venues to the country's most renowned concert halls. In December 2015, Aeham was awarded the prestigious International Beethoven Prize.

I play piano all the time. I play with orchestras in Stuttgart, Hamburg, Munich, and Berlin. It's a very big pleasure, but I don't feel good. I need to get back to Yarmouk and play piano in the street. In this dirty war, nobody can make a decision. You are dying or fleeing. You can have it only one way. And I don't have a lot of hope changing it with music. I had good memories with my music before, but now I play music with a lot of pain because I have pain. They clap for me, but those back in Syria are still in prison, under siege, under bombs.

AEHAM, A PALESTINIAN FROM SYRIA

THERE'S MORE TO THE STORY:
HTTPS://TSOSREFUGEES.ORG/BOOK/LINKS/3

My uncle said, "I can't cut off anyone's finger. I can't cut off anyone's head." They took my uncle, and he's been gone for six years.

WHEN I WAS FIVE YEARS OLD, MY FAMILY LEFT Afghanistan and went to Iran to escape the Taliban because they wanted my uncle to join them. My father was afraid they would want him, too. My uncle said, "I can't cut off anyone's finger. I can't cut off anyone's head." They took my uncle, and he's been gone for six years.

My father went back to Afghanistan four times to look for his brother. On the fourth time, he asked, "Where is my brother?" They beat him. After one week tied to the chair, they said, "If you ever come back to Afghanistan, we will kill your family and you. First we will kill your family because we want you to watch how we kill them, and in the end we will kill you."

One more time my father returned to Afghanistan, and the Taliban took my father's cousin and they cut his fingers until he died. [Parisa made a slicing motion with her hand, cutting all the way up her arm.]

Then the Iran police sent us back to Afghanistan. My father was scared. But we came back to Iran; we were smuggled. And my grandmother said to my father, "You should go to Europe."

So six months ago, we started this journey. When we got to the sea in Turkey, we stayed for three days, walking in the water up to my waist. We did not get out because of the police. When we finally did get out of the water, our clothes were very, very cold. My sister and my brother had a fever.

Now we are in Europe [Greece], but my father is still very scared and very sad. He still worries that the police here will deport him back to Afghanistan. And he worries that maybe the Taliban will find my grandmother and grandfather there.

PARISA, AFGHANISTAN

I AM AN AFGHAN WOMAN, FAMILIAR WITH PAIN AND misery since childhood, who has been carrying many bitter memories for other women. Afghanistan has nothing to do with Islam other than its name. The government is the most powerful supporter of the oppressors and the bullies. In the constitution, on paper, women have equal rights with men, but in reality they have no rights there.

Young boys are scared of the looks of brutal men, but boys are prioritized when it comes to education, purchases, food, and so on. When a boy commits a crime, his family sacrifices his sister to satisfy the family against whom the crime has been committed. If people discover a relationship between a boy and girl, they stone the girl to death and flog the boy, then release him.

A man can have up to four wives at the same time. The man is given the right to beat his wife physically. If he is divorced, the children and property will be given to the husband. If a father murders someone, he marries his daughter off to the family of the victim. If a man dies, the property will be given to his sons.

When a girl is born, all members of the family feel sad because the newborn was not a boy. An Afghan girl is not allowed to choose her own husband; he is chosen by her parents. Most women have no right to express their opinions. If a girl rejects a proposal of marriage, she can be killed, raped, or have acid put on her face.

After marriage, girls are under the control of their husbands and their in-law relatives. They must do housework like servants. The slightest failure can result in the husband beating her, tearing her nose and ears, shaving her hair, and other horrendous things. When a woman with a 100-percent-Islamic veil goes shopping, hundreds of men touch her body, and the woman feels that she should stay home. If a woman is out of her home after sunset in Kabul, people will look at her with disdain, and men will do to her whatever they can. It is wrong for a woman's voice to be heard by the neighbors. If a woman complains to the government, people will look at her as a prostitute.

Women's rights are totally trampled. In Islam, women have great value, but in Afghanistan they are not [entitled] to human rights, not true rights as taught in Islam. I am proud of our ancestors and their courage and their reputation in the world, but now Afghanistan is nothing.

I was a teacher in Afghanistan. I taught for twelve years, and I was very happy with my job. I loved it, but the problems were too great, and we couldn't live there. There was war and also tribal prejudices. There were language prejudices. Our government is Pashto, and they support Pashto

Through all of my experiences I've
learned that you can hear what a person
says with his lips, but you have to look
into his eyes to know what's in his heart.

They shot both of my knees. I was home and
totally unable to walk for two years. This,
because I wanted to help women and guide them.

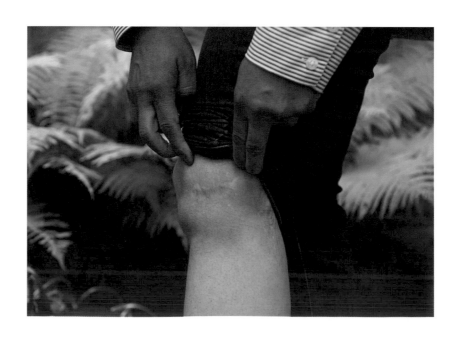

people. Whatever we tried was useless because we were Farsi speakers and Shia. In the school, children mocked each other because of religion; they insulted each other because of language. I have bad memories from there.

I worked with eight women who represented our town's women society. We would inform families, for example, of the benefits of the vaccinations for kids, and we taught them that they have rights. But one day a group of men caught me and took me to the public square and kicked me. The men persecuted me and asked, "Why do you inform our wives? You made our wives shameless and stubborn like yourself!"

They shot both of my knees. I was home and totally unable to walk for two years. This, because I wanted to help women and guide them.

We left our life there for freedom and a good future. We walked to Iran for one month. We didn't have visas, so we went illegally. We paid a lot of money to a smuggler, but he abandoned us at the border to Iran.

I'm very happy to have come out from there. Only one out of a thousand women have the courage to escape from this disastrous country. Unfortunately, they face many problems on the way, such as rape, hunger, thirst, and long walks in deep forests, plains, and mountains. They may be murdered or drown in the sea. A few manage to reach safe countries. I am one. I suffered thousands of pains and miseries and finally arrived. Not all of the problems leave. We still suffer economic and psychological problems.

I'm sure my children will have the bright futures they deserve and be good citizens. I look forward to having a calm life filled with great achievements.

Through all of my experiences I've learned that you can hear what a person says with his lips, but you have to look into his eyes to know what's in his heart.

SHAKILA, AFGHANISTAN

THERE'S MORE TO THE STORY:
HTTPS://TSOSREFUGEES.ORG/BOOK/LINKS/9

I wanted to encourage people to think freely and wisely and not to be so fanatical.

MY NAME IS TAHMINA. I AM FROM Afghanistan. I was a consultant and saleswoman for women's cosmetic products and later worked for a political party. I wanted to encourage people to think freely and wisely and not to be so fanatical. I wanted them to allow women to work, so I willingly faced the many challenges. I faced many problems when I was working; several of my female colleagues were beaten. People harassed me by throwing stones through the window of my home. I was not frightened for myself, but I was afraid that if something happened to me, my family would be persecuted too.

One day there was a suicide bombing near my home just five minutes before I left the office. My mother said we could no longer stay and must leave the country. I wasn't happy after hearing that because I wanted to stay and start a business there.

My mother traveled with four of my siblings through Pakistan into Iran. One day my mother called me and asked me to send money. She didn't tell me they were being held for ransom by smugglers because she knew I would be very worried. But I figured out what was happening to them. I had to sell things in our house quickly. Within two or three days, I collected about twenty million tomans [Iranian currency equaling nearly $5300]. I sent the money, and when my mother called me again and told me they were free, I was very happy.

I am a young girl experiencing a very difficult time in my life. I wish none of this had happened. It is not easy to start over, but I have hope for a better life.

TAHMINA, AFGHANISTAN

TWILA DAVIS BIRD, USA

TSOS chief editor

THIS IS A PHOTO OF ME AND SHAKILA, A refugee friend I've met only twice. We live a half world away from each other. When she saw me here, at our second meeting, she hugged me like she would never let go. I could feel the intensity of her gratitude for the hope she has received from our volunteer group, Their Story is Our Story (TSOS). Her fervent appreciation reminded me of a similar, despair-turned-to-hope situation in my own life.

My husband was a rising star in the field of solar physics when he was diagnosed with multiple sclerosis in his mid-thirties. He lost the use of his body quickly, was completely bedridden within five years, and lived his final twenty years as a quadriplegic. Early on, our four-level home evolved into a navigation nightmare for him. Climbing stairs sometimes required more energy and ability than he could muster; descending them became difficult and dangerous.

Before long, a personal friend confided to us that he and others were anxious to remodel our home to fit Richard's needs. We were touched but declined explaining it wasn't a project we could fund. He persisted and simply said, "The finances are already in place. If you allow us to take this project on, the rewards will be far greater on our end than yours." We finally agreed.

Early on a Saturday morning a few weeks later, a cement truck pulled up to our home and work began.

For the following two months on weeknights and Saturdays, many men who normally wore suits and ties for their day jobs donned works clothes and joined in the happy swarm of construction activity. It was a time of intense service, of intense happiness and satisfaction.

It's my turn to give back. I experience the exhilaration service brings when I'm working with refugees during their time of need just as our home-remodeling friends did when they assisted us during ours. And as they did, I've internalized the axiom, "You make a living by what you earn. You make a life by what you give."

SOPHIA BORLETTI, ITALY

SOPHIA IS ITALIAN AND HAS TRAVELED *widely with her parents. Her current home is in Paris, France, where she is a student at the American School of Paris. Because she has experienced how difficult it can be to try to fit in when coming from another country, she has a special empathy for refugees who have trouble fitting in anywhere. She has been an active member of her school's refugee-support group, Compassion Without Borders.*

I wish I could do more for the refugees here in Paris because I feel like I haven't done enough. I don't think I could ever do enough. Those children have seen what no child should ever have to see. People are taking advantage of other people's weakness. I feel so awful for them. I can't just walk by and ignore them.

I graduate in June. I'm not going to leave working with refugees behind. It's a passion I'll carry with me no matter where I go. I think about all of the love other people have given to me. It's not meant to be kept inside. It's meant to be transferred to others. Hatred can be turned into love.

KRISTI BURTON, USA

TSOS photographer

IN MY YOUTH, I MET AND BEFRIENDED A disabled man who had been brutally beaten in his youth, which resulted in a lifetime of being bound to a wheelchair with many health problems. I felt so much compassion for him; I read to him weekly for over a year.

Cruel events in my teens—the Columbine High School shooting, 9/11, the kidnapping of Elizabeth Smart, and the rape of a personal friend—further fueled my desire to alleviate suffering wherever I can among my brothers and sisters.

Refugees *are* my brothers and sisters.

FOR INFORMATION ON
HOW *YOU* CAN HELP, SEE
PAGE 228.

GARRETT GIBBONS, USA

TSOS filmmaker

I WISH THAT EVERYONE COULD SEE their ancestors and themselves in these refugees' faces.

AMY STEVENSON, USA

TSOS media packages coordinator

IN SOME WAYS THE WORLD HASN'T changed since my ancestors were forced from their homes and settled in barren, western US territory. People are still intolerant and violent. People still flee from their oppressors. People are still suspicious of those they don't know. People still seek refuge and safety. People still hope for welcome and understanding.

Charcoal drawing, TSOS artist Elizabeth Benson Thayer

I have only this one child now.
That's why we came here—so they
would not take him away from me.

MY HUSBAND HAD TWO WIVES. I WAS THE second one. When he died sixteen years ago, the first wife's children took our house, land, and everything he owned. My two sons and I fled to Pakistan. Later, we returned to ask for our share of my husband's possessions. Because of that, they killed my older son and beat Gulyar, the younger one. I hid him, then went back and buried my older son with my own hands. They beat me, too, but we escaped.

We went to Turkey and were staying with my brother, but my husband's first family called me there and sent warnings. They said they would come and kill my other son, too. I was scared. I didn't have a husband. I have only this one child now. That's why we came here—so they would not take him away from me. I just want him to be somewhere safe from his enemies. I don't want anything more. I just want him to be safe.

MINA, AFGHANISTAN

I worked as a television cameraman . . . We made a documentary movie about the Taliban and the war. When they realized what we were doing, the Taliban attacked us.

IF PEACE RETURNS TO AFGHANISTAN ONE DAY, we will definitely go back. We had a good life there. We had a house, a job, and no financial worries. We had to leave because of the war and the threat to our lives.

I worked as a television cameraman. We went to dangerous places like the Kandahar Province to report and film. We made a documentary movie about the Taliban and the war. When they realized what we were doing, the Taliban attacked us.

We fled to Iran, then Turkey, and now we are in Greece. But now we are stuck here in the hot sun. We have no freedom to move on to other countries. We don't know what our future holds for us.

FAROOSH, ELINA, AND THEIR DAUGHTER, AFGHANISTAN

They kept saying, "water, water, water."
Three people died.

MY FAMILY LOOKS TO ME TO support them. My country has no economy, no opportunity. I decided to go to Europe, but I had to go through Libya first. In the desert, we crowded onto a truck. It carried about twenty-seven people. On our way, our tire fell off. The desert was so hot. Some of our people were dying. They kept saying, "water, water, water." Three people died.

ODIJE, WESTERN AFRICA

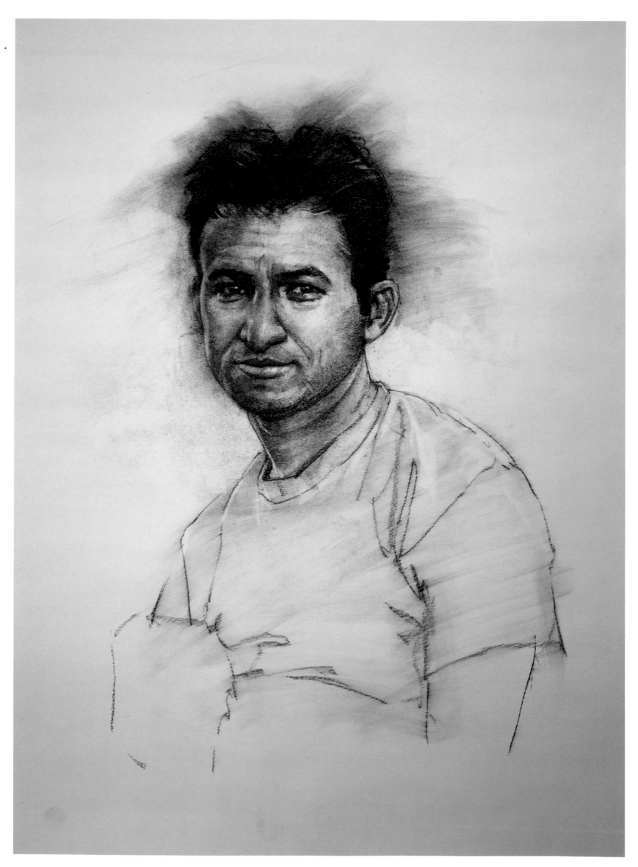

Charcoal drawing, TSOS artist Elizabeth Benson Thayer

We had to hide from the army, and in the middle of the journey, the smuggler just pointed the way we should go and left us in the mountains alone.

I AM FROM AFGHANISTAN, KUNAR PROVINCE. I AM A civil engineer. I was good at my job and had a lot of experience. The Taliban found out about me and said I must come and work with them. They would call me or send people to my village with warnings. One time, when I was driving, they attacked my car with guns. I had to jump down a steep ravine and run away. A few months later, I left Afghanistan.

I hired smugglers and travelled for many days, through Iran and Turkey and into Greece. The other refugees and I were packed into taxis, trucks, and the trunks of smugglers' cars, always barely escaping the police. We never had enough to eat, nor clean drinking water. When we stopped for the night, we couldn't sleep because there were so many people and it was so cold. When we came to the mountains, we had to continue our trip on foot through the snow.

We had to hide from the army, and in the middle of the journey, the smuggler just pointed the way we should go and left us in the mountains alone. When we eventually reached the coast, we were almost arrested before we could get to the boat that would take us across the sea to Greece. Oh God, it was so dangerous.

We finally made it to a refugee camp in Greece, and we were so happy because after such a long time we had arrived in a safe place. We thought we had made it to our goal. It was not so, and we were faced with new problems because the gates of Europe were closed tight to refugees.

After much waiting and many failed attempts, I finally managed to get to Germany. I spent eleven months in various camps in Germany. I had kidney stones, and it was hard to find treatment because I was living in a camp. Now I am better and have started language training. I hope I can find a good life and that I can continue in my profession.

NEVIN, AFGHANISTAN

I AM SIXTEEN YEARS OLD. I love clothes, I love my hair, I love shopping. I have just completed my first year in the German school. The German language isn't easy, but I did well, especially in math and science. I work hard so I can succeed here.

I often have to miss school to translate for my family at doctor's appointments and to go to the government offices to answer questions and make sure our family does everything right so we can stay here. Even though I am the youngest, I have learned German much faster than my brothers and sister, so this is my responsibility.

We laugh a lot, but I also worry. My mother and I have been told we won't be deported for now, but my three older brothers received a notice that they would be deported within thirty days. I had to quickly find a lawyer to appeal the German government's decision for them. Now we pay a lawyer each month, but it is worth it, because if my brothers have to go back, it will be very dangerous for them.

I want my family to stay together here where we can be safe. I want to go to school, to dress how I want, to make decisions for myself. My goal is to study at a university. I like it here. I want to stay.

NORINA, AFGHAN FROM IRAN

I want to go to school, to dress how I want, to make decisions for myself. My goal is to study at a university. I like it here. I want to stay.

The water we had was pink. We could not drink it because it was rotten. To drink it was to die. Some people, however, did drink it because there was no water.

I AM FROM NIGERIA, AND I HAVE A FAMILY BACK HOME. MY DAD HAS seven children. My mom gave him five children. I left home about two months after coming back from a two-year mission for our church. Then my family supported me to go learn and work because of the love they have for me. They gave money to send me to Europe for school to study computer engineering. My family loves me so much.

I traveled to Congo then to Niger and to Libya. Before we got to Libya, there was a lot of struggling in the desert. They took about twenty-nine or thirty of us in the back of a truck, and the smugglers told us if we didn't sit tight while the motor was moving, we could fall, and if we fell, the driver would not wait. One friend died in the desert. We had to pay bribes to border guards to pass through the land. And we had to pay money to eat. The little we had was expensive. Many women died in the camp, where we slept on the ground like slaves. Many people died. A lot. The water we had was pink. We could not drink it because it was rotten. To drink it was to die. Some people, however, did drink it because there was no water. That journey is very, very risky.

When we reached the sea, we were held captive for money. The Arab people did not want us to go outside or to go for a walk. They could shoot you or send you back home. I spent nine months in Libya calling my parents every month to get more money. A man kept pushing me for money. My mom sent me 100,000 euro, and I had to give it to the man that was pushing people and they released me. In Libya, life is no good.

Government people rescued us when we were far out at sea on our way to Italy. We pushed out five boats; four capsized during the journey. A lot of souls died in that sea. There were people calling for their children—their son, their daughter. The others would lie, "They aren't here; we do not have them. They are not dead." For so long they were calling. Hoping. Not knowing they had died.

The first day I came to Italy, I had a friend, an Italian friend. I told her I want to locate a church to go to. She said she would help me find it. I told her I was a missionary. Finally we found one here, so from that time I have been able to attend the church.

FELIX, NIGERIA

I LEFT HOME WHEN I WAS ABOUT fourteen because of religious conflict and violence. Our way of living in Africa is different from the Western world. We are not used to a police system or police people who protect citizens. If you have money, you are safe. If not, you are powerless.

My family is from West Africa. My mom was from the southern part of our country; my dad was from the northern part. In the north, most people are Muslims. If a Muslim wants to marry a Christian or convert to Christianity, it's difficult. The Muslims there didn't allow my dad to convert to Christianity, so he never did.

Several years ago, my father took me to visit his parents in the north. One day, early in the morning, a fight broke out in the community and two people died. Some people came to my dad's house. They had a gun and killed my father. They said, "He married a Christian. Where is his bastard? We want to kill him so we finish off the family." I was taking my shower. The bathroom and tub were outside the house. I just tied my towel around me and I ran to the road. Alongside the road, I stopped a car and was crying. In our country, if you see someone who is in difficulty, if you know him or not, you help. The man asked me, "What has happened?" I explained. He took me to a border town, and I stayed with him. Then he took me to Libya, and I found a job before going on to Italy.

I have come to seek asylum. I want to continue my education and go to school to be a barber. I want to support myself and live my life as my own.

I wanted to stay in Africa, but I wanted my life to be secure, so I came to Europe.

HEYDI, WEST AFRICA

They said, "He married a Christian. Where is his bastard? We want to kill him so we finish off the family."

Papa started to drive the boat. He was worried about all of us. Men came and took him away. I haven't seen him since.

I CAME ON A BOAT. IT WAS A big boat. It had so many people in it! The bad men who took our money jumped into the water and left us. Water was coming in the boat and we were getting wet. Papa started to drive the boat. He was worried about all of us. Men came and took him away. I haven't seen him since.

NOODA, SYRIA

Based on interview with Nooda's mother

I just want to live in a safe
place where everyone can
live united and in peace,
whether they be Shia, Sunni,
Christian or whatever.

BECAUSE WE ARE SHIA AND THE
Taliban are Sunni, they want to destroy us.
My sister was forced to marry into a Taliban
family. They killed her. Our uncle helped
finance our escape. We now have no contact
with our family in Afghanistan.

I just want to live in a safe place where
everyone can live united and in peace,
whether they be Shia, Sunni, Christian or
whatever.

MADINA, AFGHANISTAN

They said, "Call your family.
Send money." I said, "I don't have
family. I am an orphan."

I WAS BORN IN SOMALIA. ONE DAY, WHEN I was nine years old, I came home from school and saw too many people at my house. When I went inside, I saw my father, my mother, my six sisters, and four brothers were all dying. Someone killed my family. I don't know why.

My uncle took me to live in Yemen; I lived there with him until I was sixteen years old. Then I decided to go to Europe. I went through Libya to get to the sea. But the militia took me to a prison for seven months. They said, "Call your family. Send money." I said, "I don't have family. I am an orphan." But he said, "*No!* Call them." I said, "I don't have a family to call." After that, he beat me until I was very sick, and I was in the hospital for three months.

In Libya, I saw sisters and brothers who were abused by the military. They would take the girls and do sex with them by force. If we tried to help, they would kill us. There's no justice. It is a desperate life.

I finally left Libya and went to Sweden to get a good life. I stayed there six years, but I was not happy. I remembered all the things that happened to me. Now I'm in Italy.

I am always stressed about memories of my family and war. I don't know how to be happy. I see my family in my eyes, and I don't know what to do. I am not strong. I speak five languages. I need to work so I won't just think about my family anymore.

MoMo, Somalia

They say girls have no right to study or work or protest. Twice we were poisoned and our mother had to take us from school to the hospital.

MY SISTERS AND I WERE IN secondary school in Afghanistan, but our community leaders were not happy about this. They say girls have no right to study or work or protest. Twice we were poisoned and our mother had to take us from school to the hospital. After that, she kept us home because of the insecurity. She brought us out of Afghanistan to go to a better country where we can continue our studies and live in security. It is my wish to resume my education.

Shurangez has spent the last three years in camps attempting to cross borders to a country where she can finally continue her education. She and her mother, brothers, and sisters are currently trapped in Serbia with no means to move forward, and they cannot go back.

SHURANGEZ, AFGHANISTAN

KELVIN BELCHER, ENGLAND

I'M KELVIN, FROM BRISTOL, ENGLAND.
I'm a long-term volunteer, collecting supplies people donate and distributing them to people in need. We connect with other people and other aid groups on Facebook to try and get the word out and get the work done. We call our group "Paris Refugee Ground Support."

The mainstream media portrays these people as faceless refugees. They're coming here to take your welfare. They're coming here for your social housing. They're coming here for your jobs. But they are people like you and me. They are families. They are mothers. They are fathers. They have children. They care about their quality of life. We are all global brothers and sisters. We've just forgotten that because we've been so isolated within borders and within nations.

Think about the situation if it was reversed, and think how you would want to be received, how you would want to be protected, and how you would want your families to be protected.

It's not all about the big things. It's the little things that make a difference as well—on a personal level. There's always something someone can do, no matter how small. Not everyone can do what we're doing. Not everyone can be in the field, on the ground giving stuff. But everyone can help If you really want to help, there's always a way.

TARAH WESTOVER, USA

TSOS transcription coordinator

AS THE REFUGEE CRISIS UNFOLDED, I
felt a pull to become involved. I decided I wanted to work with the refugees, so I moved to Greece. The specific population I worked with was a high-risk and fragile population of pregnant women and children under the age of two. I've always had a great love and appreciation for diverse cultures and beliefs and the Syrian people were no exception. I fell in love. Immediately. As I heard their stories, I asked myself constantly, "Why this? Why them? Why children? Why families? Why at all? Why to anyone?" Words on a page cannot adequately express what happened inside my heart as I spent time building relationships with these refugees. It was such a privilege to love and to be loved by them, especially in such a fragile and trying time of hurt, persecution, sickness, death and fear. Their capacity to love, accept, forgive, rebuild and trust inspired me every single day. I feel a responsibility to help others hear their stories and understand who these people are. They love deeply. They give unselfishly. They worship devoutly. They can teach us a thing or two. They are my dearest friends. It's my hope that through the efforts of TSOS, more people can begin to understand that their stories are no different than our own.

ELIZABETH THAYER, USA

TSOS artist coordinator

HAVING BEEN A "STRANGER IN A strange land" myself, having ancestors who were forced from their homes, believing in a God to whom all people are equally precious, and having won the lottery of birth, I feel I cannot turn my back on others who have been forced from their homes. I want to help. My goal is to advocate for refugees by creating a space in which people can come face to face with the crisis and with individuals, and perhaps experience a change in perspective. Art has the power to bring people together in a shared experience, to overcome prejudices, and to reteach the act of seeing. I hope that my work will help others understand the challenges refugees face, encourage empathy, and inspire others to find their own way to come to the rescue.

FOR INFORMATION ON HOW *YOU* CAN HELP, SEE PAGE 228.

KAYRA MARTINEZ, GREECE

I HAVE BEEN A FLIGHT ATTENDANT FOR twenty-five years, and for most of that time my life consisted of traveling, fine dining, arts, and theater. Everything was about me. I was living in Frankfurt when refugees started coming in the summer of 2015, and they needed donations of clothing. When I dropped off my first carload of clothes and shoes, I asked, "May I stay and help?" Organizers said, "Absolutely." After that, I just kept volunteering.

Eventually, I went to Greece and volunteered at the Nea Kavala camp. I created a nonprofit called Nea Kavala Art Without Borders. We sell art created by refugees. We're using this art to create support for the families and to help the children work through their trauma. We want to give displaced people some independence, some empowerment, and a way to make their own living. We have refugees making things like paintings, jewelry, and baby clothes. All the money earned goes to the artists.

This project started with children. We took a dozen children out of the camps where I was working and brought them to my house. We gave them each a canvas and explained they could draw whatever they wanted. In the beginning, the drawings were always about their journey from Turkey to Greece across the Aegean Sea. I think they saw a lot of death, a lot of devastation during this time. But as time went on, most of the drawings were full of hope and love. To me, that is success.

Because I am almost fourteen and the oldest son, I am responsible for our family. I decided to leave on my own and make my way to Germany.

MY FATHER WAS A MEMBER OF THE TALIBAN. MY mother was forced to marry him. We are seven children—three boys and four girls. When the Taliban came into our village, my mother took us into the mountains to hide for days. This happened many times.

When my father was killed, his family wanted to marry off my three older sisters and force my mother to remarry. My mother refused. The village where we lived wouldn't let any of us go to school, and they wouldn't give my mother work because they knew my father was Taliban.

My mother's family was different. My uncle went to Germany. He sent us money, and that is how we survived. He told my mother to come join him and gave us enough money to pay for her and four of us to go to Germany with her. My mother was forced to make a decision. She had to decide which of her seven children to take with her and which to leave behind. She decided to take the four youngest and leave my three older sisters in the care of our aunt, my father's sister. My mother hasn't been the same since. She can't sleep, she can't eat—she is constantly worried about my sisters and tormented by her guilt.

We made it as far as Greece. For two years we lived in a tent in a camp near Athens because the borders to Europe and Germany were closed. We were able to talk to my sisters back in Afghanistan once in a while. My father's family kept threatening to sell them. My mother sent as much money as she could to keep them safe.

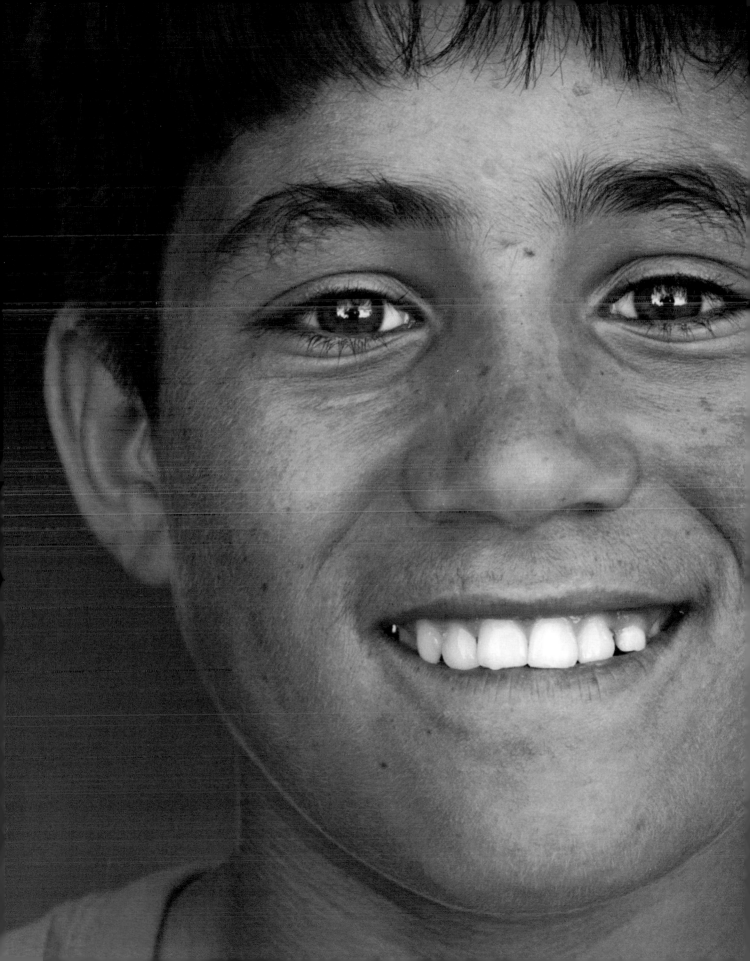

Then my mother received a phone call from my father's family. One of my sisters had disappeared. My mother was frantic. Had they sold her? Was she safe? Did she run away? A few weeks later, she received another phone call. They had found my sister. Her mutilated body had been delivered to the village with a delivery of grain.

My mother went into our tent, curled up in a ball, and didn't come out for three months.

Because I am almost fourteen and the oldest son, I am responsible for our family. I decided to leave on my own and make my way to Germany. I figured if I could find my uncle, he could help me find a way to make enough money to bring my two older sisters who are still in Afghanistan to us. Then my mother would be happy again.

I made my way all the way up through Italy, through Austria, and finally crossed the border into Germany. It wasn't easy, and I saw some terrible things. But I made it! My uncle and I are in contact but not allowed to live together. Now I am in a home with other boys who don't have their parents with them. I try to call my mother as often as I can. She is doing better. Through the help of others, she and my younger brothers and sister have an apartment in Athens.

I am going to school. I am learning to speak German. There are people here who want to help me. I hope our family will be together again soon.

OMAR, AFGHANISTAN

IN A US-FUNDED PROJECT, MUSA HELPED create a database of Afghan military personnel. He also helped identify terrorist spies, which put his own life in danger. He was attacked twice. Once an RPG fired directly at his car went through one window and out the other without injury to the passengers. He wasn't as lucky the second time. A terrorist on a passing motorbike attached a magnet bomb to his car. The resulting explosion propelled Musa through the windshield. He barely survived. His bodyguards were killed.

Musa, his wife and baby, his parents, and his brother fled from Afghanistan after having survived these two bomb attacks and a separate one directed at his father. They have spent two years trying (unsuccessfully) to find a place to live in the European Union.

Musa's face and name have been altered for his and his family's safety.

We were a rich family in Afghanistan. I had a car. My dad had a car, a private house, plenty of income each month. My dad was a civil engineer and was earning enough. My mom was working. I was working. So economically, there was no problem at all. Nothing. We are not here for economic reasons. We are not here for vacation. We are not here for having fun. We are here to seek safety.

I'm educated. I know five languages. I have skills. My wife has skills. My mom has skills. My dad has skills. We can use them. I don't want economic support from any other country. I just need security. I just need peace. I just need to live.

Once I was playing with life, I was enjoying life, but now life is playing with me. I don't know what my destiny will be.

MUSA, AFGHANISTAN

Oil on linen, TSOS artist Elizabeth Benson Thayer

No one secs my pain.
No one knows my loss.
I am invisible.

The war had begun where we were. The bombs demolished our house and my uncle's house.

OUR LIFE WAS VERY GOOD. WE WERE VERY comfortable and happy. One day we went to sleep and awoke to find the planes bombing above us. The war had begun where we were. The bombs demolished our house and my uncle's house. My uncle died in the attack. So we left for Turkey.

In Turkey my husband began working, but they didn't pay him for his work. We began to go hungry. My husband left before I did because we didn't have the money to leave with him. After a while my children and I left, and I also brought my husband's younger brother with me. I was five months pregnant. I suffered a lot on the way.

We came by sea, and the smugglers abandoned us on a deserted island. We took off our life jackets and set them on fire to get warm. My children suffered with me. They were exhausted. They even got sick in their chests from the cold winds. We begged passing fishermen to rescue us. When we paid them money, they took us off the island.

I gave birth in a refugee camp and remained there for two months. I kept asking that they bring me, my husband, and my children back together. For months they told me, "You need to wait in court." In the end they sent me to a house where many other women and their children lived. I have one room for me and my family.

My husband and I are in the same country but in different cities. In the city where he is, my husband had his younger sister with him. When they saw her not laughing in school and looking sad, they took her away from my husband. Now she lives far from him and is much more sad, so sad she won't eat. She wants to live with her brother, but they won't let her.

We came from being under attack, and we still feel alienated here. We hope that after all this, our family will be back together for the sake of all these children.

SANAZ, SYRIA

ELIZABETH THAYER:

I met Saedah in Germany and was enchanted by her bright, light blue eyes and sweet temperament. She was living in one home with twenty-six other women and children who had been separated from husbands and fathers somewhere along their flight to safety. They are among the eleven million Syrians who have fled their homes, hoping to escape the horrors of war and find some kind of peace. It is a crisis that will not just go away. Millions of normal, everyday people are sitting in temporary housing, refugee camps, or worse, waiting for life to begin again.

I kept the brushwork in this painting loose and expressive, hoping to convey the turmoil and upheaval so many young people are experiencing at an early stage in their lives. They live in uncertainty but are remarkably resilient and cheerful in bad conditions. They hold up the best they can and cling to the most important things—loved ones, faith, and hope. They are Holding On.

HOLDING ON

Oil on canvas, TSOS artist Elizabeth Benson Thayer

I GRADUATED WITH A DEGREE IN JOURNALISM and joined the Afghan police force. I was responsible for their media. When we joined forces with NATO, I worked as a television journalist with them for four years. My duty was to shoot videos during operations with the NATO forces and also during opium raids and anti-terrorist campaigns.

I lost many of my friends during these operations. Ahmad, who worked with me, was caught by terrorists, and they tore his skin apart. They said it was because he cooperated with the government. Abolfazl was killed when he left his home to go to his point of service. Reshad was killed when he was going to his bank. Eghbal was shot in the eye when he went to Shindel Market to buy a CD and listen to music. Mir Veis, who was responsible for detecting mines for three years, was exploded by a mine and died. When I took his dead body to his house, his fiancée went mad.

These incidents all happened while we were trying to bring peace to Afghanistan, destroy narcotics, and kill terrorists. That was our responsibility and why we joined the police and received special training.

I was tired of losing my friends during war, so after four years of duty, I quit. I began working as an announcer on a local radio station, but I began getting warnings from the Taliban. They said they would kill me because I had produced media against them, so I fled to Pakistan. Then I heard they had found my family and killed my father. I could not go back. I decided to continue on my way to Iran, then Turkey, then Greece.

Now I have been here for months, and I don't know what will happen. I am trying to seek asylum, but there are many problems and nothing is clear. They don't give us answers.

WALID, AFGHANISTAN

I began working as an announcer on a local radio station, but I began getting warnings from the Taliban. . . . so I fled to Pakistan. Then I heard they had found my family and killed my father. I could not go back.

I AM FORTY-TWO YEARS OLD. WE HAVE been at war in Afghanistan for forty-five years! Since I was born and throughout my life I have known conflict and war. I have been living in war my whole life.

In Afghanistan, suicide attacks and car bombs were our hidden enemies. We didn't know where they would be. Under a car, on a bike, in the street—they could be anywhere. We couldn't run from something we couldn't see. We lost friends. They would lose a hand or a leg or be killed. We lost our families. It could happen any time—we couldn't know when. This is the worst kind of war.

I don't want my children to live in war. We just want to be safe. We just want peace.

LARIF, AFGHANISTAN

THERE'S MORE TO THE STORY:
HTTPS://TSOSREFUGEES.ORG/BOOK/LINKS/4

I don't want my children to live in war.
Wc just want to be safe. We just want peace.

Nine months pregnant, I boarded a plane and within minutes flew over those impassible borders into Germany. I gave birth to our fifth child alone.

MY HUSBAND IS RAISING OUR THREE daughters and our son in a camp in Greece without me. He is a good man. He is an engineer, a schoolteacher, and an artist. We love each other, and we love our children. That is why I had to leave, to give our family the hope of a better life. After two years of fighting to keep our family together and safe, after two years of dirty camps and dangerous border crossings, after two years of running into closed doors, we decided it was time to separate.

Nine months pregnant, I boarded a plane and within minutes flew over those impassible borders into Germany. I gave birth to our fifth child alone. Every day I pray this daughter will never know the fear our other children have experienced. I yearn for the day my husband will hold this daughter in his arms and our family will be together again.

No more running, no more danger, no more barriers—together and safe—that is our hope for ourselves and our children. This is why I had to leave.

After more than two years of camps and attempted border crossings as a family, Mohida traveled alone to Germany in the hopes that she could pull them in after her through family reunification.

MOHIDA, AFGHANISTAN

I am thirteen. I want to go back to school. I want to have a room with a bed and space to breathe. I want to be safe again.

WE LEFT OUR HOME AFTER THE TALIBAN beat my father and made him quit his job. They threatened to torture and kill my sisters, my brother, and me. So we left.

I have seen many countries now. I have walked through Iran and Turkey. I have lived in Greece, walked through Macedonia and Albania, and lived in Serbia. We tried many times to get into Romania. It was very cold, and we walked all night in the mountains and had to be fast and quiet. We were caught and sent back every time. Now we are back in a camp in Greece.

I am thirteen. I want to go back to school. I want to have a room with a bed and space to breathe. I want to be safe again.

MARIAM, AFGHANISTAN

Based on an interview with Mariam's father.

MY FATHER IS A SCHOOLTEACHER, BUT
we have no school in the camp. My sisters, my brother,
and I haven't been in school for three years, now.

MALIA, AFGHANISTAN

Based on an interview with Malia's father.

MY MOMMY HAD A BABY IN HER tummy, then she said goodbye and left. I see Mommy on Daddy's phone. She talks to us, and I see the baby. It's a girl. She gets to be with Mommy. I don't. Daddy says they are in Germany and we have to wait here in Greece for people to let us be together again.

GOMAL, AFGHANISTAN

Based on an interview with Gomal's father.

TSOS co-executive director

IN THE SUMMER OF 2016, WHEN I READ a newspaper article about a refugee camp being set up close to my home with fifty small mobile homes, I organized a neighborhood group to help meet the residents' needs. We met in a neighborhood cafe regularly to organize and plan.

We set up German classes, craft sessions, community trips, cooking classes, school tutoring, and a small lending library. With help from the refugees, we built lounge furniture for a community tent and set up a bicycle repair shop. We also tried to get to know their culture and expose them to ours.

At Christmas they helped us decorate a Christmas tree, which was entirely new to Syrians and Afghans. We had an awesome party with lots of food, music, and presents. An elderly Syrian man said, "You know, I want to go back to my home, but I want to collect good memories to take back with me. This is one of the best memories I've had so far."

Most camp residents experienced great trauma before coming to Germany. They need professional help but also support from friends. They need to be able to open up and talk about their sorrows without someone next to them being totally afraid of what they're hearing. They need a listening ear and compassion; they need someone who can express sorrow for what they have gone through and reassure them they are safe.

My work at the camp had a positive influence on my young son. Seeing that has helped me decide what I want to do with my life. I want to be a good role model for my kids and show them what is most important in the world. It's about compassion. It's about helping other people. It's not about yourself and how much money you earn or what kind of job you have or what kind of car you drive. It's about who you are. In the end you will be judged by the fullness of your heart. That's what I'm trying to teach my kids.

PHOEBE WOOD, FRANCE

TSOS journalist and videographer

AS A JOURNALIST, I TRAVELED TO ITALY where I met a group of refugees, all strangers to one another, who had been thrown into an unfamiliar situation and told to make it work. Though many of them were from the African continent, they had a whole range of mother tongues and were all trying to speed-learn Italian in order to have a mutual language. This collective action was so inspiring, it made me yearn for a greater acceptance in the world so that refugees like those I met can feel welcome in their new homes.

TSOS photographer coordinator

MY GRANDFATHER WAS A FRENCH OFFICER during World War II. After surviving strong fighting on the mainland and intense strafing by German Stuka planes on Dunkirk beach, my grandfather was rescued and boarded a boat to go to England. On the boat deck, he saw a soldier who was in shock and crying. The private, who had no life jacket, told him he didn't know how to swim. My grandfather, who was a great swimmer, gave him the life jacket he had been issued as an officer.

Recently, a former client told me that during this past year, as refugees surged into France, she had wondered what to do for them. With her husband, they agreed to be a host family for a refugee and became friends with that man until the day he was sent back to his country with little consideration by authorities for all his efforts to learn the French language and integrate into our culture. To this day, the host family has had no news from him and they're wondering how he is doing in his mother country.

When I asked her why they got involved as a host family, she answered after a pause, "What will we answer our kids if one day they ask us, 'What did you do to help refugees?'"

Like my grandfather, who gave away his officer's life jacket, we might all be confronted with a situation where we have to choose between denying someone in desperate need a life-saving kindness or sharing our abundant privileges. The question keeps coming into my mind, "Who will I give my life jacket to?"

JORDAN GREEN PFAU, USA

TSOS data specialist

A FEW YEARS AGO, MY FAMILY relocated to Japan, far away from our American roots; we were unable to speak the language and felt very much like outsiders. It gave me just a small taste of how refugees must feel when they find themselves in a completely new place so far from their homes.

Yet how different our circumstances. With the uncertainty and chaos in the world, however, it feels like at any moment this could be the situation for any of us.

> FOR INFORMATION ON
>
> HOW *YOU* CAN HELP, SEE
>
> PAGE 228.

MY NAME IS HAMED. I AM FROM AFGHANISTAN, IN KABUL. I
have an MA in international relations and diplomacy from Kabul University.
I worked with the US Army as an interpreter. When the American troops left
Afghanistan, the lives of all the interpreters were in danger. We were very well
known, and many times we were threatened by the Taliban. That's why I decided
to leave Afghanistan.

I came only with my wife and daughter. We hired smugglers to take us through
Iran and Turkey, and then across the sea to Greece. The smugglers who took us
to the boat, they were not human at all. They don't value the lives of the refugees.
They simply make a lot of money and put us at great risk. We all knew that if we
got on this boat, we could die. But we didn't have any other option. So we paid for
our death. You cannot imagine how dangerous it was in that boat! All this way I
kept praying for my family. And I imagined what I would do if the boat collapsed.
How many people could I save? I probably couldn't even save my own daughter,
my own wife. It was very difficult. But fortunately, like a miracle, we were rescued
while crossing that sea, and we came to Greece.

We were in a good camp in Greece with many facilities that other camps don't
have—a school, good food, clean water, and electricity. But we didn't come for all
of that. We wanted to go to a country where we could start a new life, a new
future. I felt trapped there. When I saw my daughter in this situation, I would
think, "What is going to happen to my daughter? She is now two years old. If she
grows up and we are still here—there is no point." So after almost a year of living
there, we decided to leave.

We wanted to go to Serbia because we heard that it was possible for some
people to legally cross the border into Hungary. We tried to go through Macedonia,
then through Albania. We walked for days through hills and forests, farmlands,
and mountains. Once we had to follow a train track through a dark tunnel and
over a bridge, and we had to run to find a safe place if we heard a train coming.
When we finally managed to get to a refugee camp in Serbia, conditions were very
bad. So many refugees come to Serbia in the hope that one day they will cross
to Hungary and then make it to Austria or Germany. But their names never get
picked, and over time they lose hope. For myself, Serbia was a kind of hell. So we
tried again and again to get over the border into Croatia, or Hungary, or Romania.
We were always sent back. Sometimes the police were cruel and they stole our
money and our phones and our medicine. We had to keep quiet about it or they
would make trouble for us. Finally, after a year in Serbia, we decided to just go
back to Greece and try something else.

Our next plan was to try to go to Switzerland by plane. My wife and daughter
went through the gate onto the plane with no problem, but I was stopped and
had to go back. I had a choice then—whether to call them back so we could stay
together, or to let them go on without me. I didn't want to send them on alone, but
I thought things would be better for them in Switzerland, so I let them go. It was
very hard for my wife. In Switzerland, she had to stay in a room with eight other

So we paid for our death. You cannot imagine
how dangerous it was in that boat! How many
people could I save? I probably couldn't even
save my own daughter, my own wife.

people. My daughter was crying for me all the time, and she started biting herself and getting sick, and the other people got very angry that my wife couldn't keep her quiet. I tried again and again to get to Switzerland to be with them, but I was always caught and sent back. I was so discouraged that I was about to tell them to come back to Greece, or even say that we should all go back to Afghanistan. But I thought I would try once more. This time, I made it, and I am so happy that we are all together in a country where we can start to build a new life again. When I look back now at all that has happened, I feel like all the troubles we had in Serbia were really a blessing in disguise, because eventually they brought us here.

We haven't been granted asylum yet, but I am very hopeful that soon I will have a job and we will move into our own home. We go regularly to German classes, and my wife works at the kindergarten where my daughter goes to school. I am very optimistic about our future life here, especially for my daughter. Here she will have a good life, a peaceful life. There are many opportunities here, and we have to take them. I didn't come to Switzerland in order to just eat or sleep or be dependent on charity organizations or on the government. No. I'm educated. I can learn the language quickly. I can find a job, and I will pay my taxes and make a real life and a real contribution here. Here, we have to rebuild our lives and try to regain all that we have lost over the last two years. Here, we have to begin at the beginning.

My family and I went through many troubles and difficulties on our way here. But I kept thinking one day we will have a better life. I had to fight to hold on to my hope. And now when I turn and see my family, I'm so glad I didn't give up. I kept hope alive in my heart. It kept me moving. I couldn't let myself be overwhelmed by disappointment, so I fought to keep my hope. I always tried to do my best for my family, and now I think, "I have done something for them!"

There are many thousands of people making this journey, just like us. All these refugees want to come to a safe place to experience a better life, but right now every door is closed to them. This is a shame. I have many, many friends who are still trapped in Serbia, and they are very discouraged because the conditions there are so bad. It is so difficult for me when I think of them and all that they are still going through. It gives me a bad feeling to know that I am safe and my friends are still in trouble. I want to do something. I will use all my chances, all my resources that I have here to try to help them.

In January 2017, a large group of Afghan refugees our TSOS team had interviewed in Greece a few months previously struck out together for Serbia, where they hoped to improve their chances for gaining entrance to Germany or Sweden. Eleven families, with twenty-nine children in tow, walked over 300 miles through Macedonia and up into wintry Serbia. Many of them literally walked the soles off their shoes, arriving sick and exhausted.

TSOS team members in Germany discovered their plight, assembled suitcases full of shoes, and sent them to the exhausted refugee families. Hamed wrote back:

My tears are running down and remind me that we are not really alone in this bad situation and massive world. All I know is God sends real persons to fight for us and to help keep hope in a bright future. We believe there are angels surrounding us even from far away that consider us and assist us even though we don't know them. All these families are hoping people will listen to our stories and the problems we have. We want to wake up the sleeping conscience!

HAMED ARIAN, AFGHAN IN SWITZERLAND

TSOS refugee coordinator

I had to fight to hold on to my hope. And now when I turn and see my family, I'm so glad I didn't give up.

THERE'S MORE TO THE STORY:
HTTPS://TSOSREFUGEES.ORG/BOOK/LINKS/6

I AM NABI, AND I'M TWENTY-FIVE YEARS OLD. I finished my bachelor's degree as an engineer, and now I am a refugee in Germany. I am also homosexual. It was hard to be gay in my country. You can't live as a [free] man. I heard about the Taliban taking gay men and slaughtering them like animals. But the main reason I left Afghanistan was because of my sister. The Taliban wanted to stone her, so we left together.

We came through Iran in the summer, when it was very hot—115 degrees Fahrenheit. We were out in the open the whole time. Some of the people in our group died because we didn't have water. From Iran, we went on to Turkey, and [then] to Greece. After that we traveled for four months on foot through Macedonia, Serbia, and so on until we got to Germany.

I spent a year and a half living in the Rebstockbad camp. At first I didn't want to learn German. Then I met a German man online, and he visited me. We started dating, and he has helped me learn German. We write notes to each other, we do household chores, we go shopping, and we visit his parents, all the time speaking German as much as we can.

Now I have an apartment in Frankfurt, and I have a job so I can pay my bills, and it feels like I have my life back again. I am also helping others like me. There is a group called Rainbow Refugees for gay men from Afghanistan and Pakistan. I help them with the language, I explain the laws to them, and I help them be more open about who they are.

For now, I try my best to learn German well enough to get an internship in engineering and continue my studies. I hope I can live like a normal man here, as a free gay man. And I hope that I can stay with my boyfriend and we can develop a life together, because we love each other.

NABI, AFGHANISTAN

I heard about the Taliban taking
gay men and slaughtering them
like animals.

HELLO TO EVERYONE WHO IS listening to my story. My name is Shekib, and I came to Germany when I was seventeen years old. Now I am nineteen. I am a refugee here in Germany.

The German government has rejected my asylum request, and I don't know what should I do. They gave a temporary status to my family so that they can stay here, but they rejected me.

If they send me back to Afghanistan or any other country, what will I do?

I have not seen Afghanistan in my life. Because my parents fled Afghanistan to Iran before I was born, I have never known the country of my heritage. But I heard there is a country called Afghanistan. There is a place called Kabul, the capital of Afghanistan. This is a place where every day people are losing their lives in explosions. I have not been to Afghanistan yet, but if the German government deports me to Afghanistan, what will be my future? I cannot live with fear in my life about Afghanistan. Fear of going outside and you don't know when or where a bomb next to you will explode. I really can't live with this fear.

The only thing I have in my life is my mother. My father died when I was very young, leaving my mother to raise us on her own. Although she can't read or write, she is wise and strong and solid. If she cannot be with me, I do not want this life anymore. Life doesn't make sense if my mother is not with me. I will kill myself and end my life if they separate me from my mother.

SHEKIB, AFGHAN FROM IRAN

BAROS COMES FROM A COASTAL VILLAGE IN WEST *Africa. Illegal, large-scale mining of the village's coastline for valuable minerals has endangered the livelihood and lives of local residents for years. Mining operations have not only posed a threat to tourism, which relies on unspoiled coastal beaches, but have also destroyed vast acres of farmland. The mining has also triggered soil erosion, and created stagnant, flooded ditches, which then become breeding grounds for mosquitoes and habitats for crocodiles. Villagers adjacent to the damaged areas are put at risk. Baros was among dozens who protested the mining activities and confronted truckers at the site in the fall of 2015. They threw stones, smashed windshields, and vandalized mining company property. Many were arrested and tortured.*

We tried to protect and fight for our right to stop those kinds of things from happening. It's not good for our village. We had to stand and fight for our right to stop the big trucks from sand mining. When we did, we had a problem with PIU [police intervention unit] officers. There were a lot of people arrested for that issue. This is the reason why I left my country.

I worked for a while in Senegal, then I went to Libya with one of my coworkers because he said we could get work there. One day I came from work and I was attacked by gunmen—you know, they were looking for money. In the struggle with them, I lost three teeth. Now, when I talk to my family with my phone, I turn off the video because I don't want them to see my teeth and feel sad.

Now I am in Italy. I've been here for over one year now. It's hard for us [people from Africa] to live here. I don't think the Italians feel we are the same as them. It's because of our color. But color is only color. Are we not human beings?

BAROS, WEST AFRICA

Color is only color. Are we not
human beings?

. . . my father began telling me I must join this
society but I told him I was a Christian, that I
could not follow him.

MY HOME WAS IN WEST AFRICA. I LEFT BECAUSE I had a problem. My father is a society man*. It was my mother who told me my father was a society man, but I didn't believe her. I was close to my mother. She was a Christian and always took me to church.

My father didn't allow me to enter his room, but he would give my mother a key to the room so she could go in and clean. One day when she was sweeping, she saw documents from the society. She told me about them, and then I believed her.

When I was eighteen years-old, my father began telling me I must join this society but I told him I was a Christian, that I could not follow him. He threatened me and used many persuasive words. But I did not want to join the society. My father became angry and began beating me until I was bloody.

When my mother saw that my father wanted to kill me, she took me out of the house to a nurse and left me there. When she returned home, my father asked her where I was. Then my mother left my father and didn't return because she didn't want me to die.

When I could walk again, I left my country to save my life. I will never go back. Now I am here in Italy. My hope is to find welding work. I want to begin a good life here.

*"Secret societies or cults exist in West African countries, but, by their nature, very little is known about them. The most widely reported and studied is the Ogboni Society, which is strongly associated with those with money and power. Members use their influence to ensure affairs in government and society are favorable to their desires. An individual whose father is a member of this society would be expected to join and sometimes pressure to do so has been considered life threatening." (Report researched and compiled by the Refugee Documentation Centre of Ireland in June 2010.)

GODSPOWER, WEST AFRICA

When the police searched her bag, they found her copy of the book. They realized it was a Christian book, so they took her to the police station, questioned her, tortured her, and put her in jail.

FREEDOM OF RELIGION—NOT EVERYONE HAS IT.

My friends and I lived in an Islamic country, but we always had problems with Islam. I received a Christian book from someone, and I made copies of it so my friends and I could read it. We studied it together for one or two months. Then one of my friends got arrested in a park. When the police searched her bag, they found her copy of the book. They realized it was a Christian book, so they took her to the police station, questioned her, tortured her, and put her in jail. She finally gave them my name. When the police came to my home, I was not there, thank God. I was at my uncle's house. I could not go back home. I was able to escape.

I walked all the way to Turkey [over 1600 miles]. I had no money. I had to work in long shifts in a restaurant until I finally earned enough money to finish my journey to Germany. I arrived here barefoot and in very bad condition. I found the father of the person who gave me the Christian book and went to visit him. I explained to him what had happened to me, told him that I knew his son, and how I received the book from him. After that he spent a lot of time with me. I converted to Christianity.

I cannot go back, I really cannot. If that had been an option, I would not have tolerated these three years since I left—three years of extremely dire conditions and loneliness. I went to court and explained everything truthfully. In spite of that, they want to deport me back to my country. I cannot go back, I cannot.

Loneliness grows and turns into an obsession in the heart because my family is not with me. I will keep trying to implore God to help me in this difficult situation and to guide me in the right path for a good life here.

SAHAR, A MIDDLE EASTERN COUNTRY

ASAD AND HIS OLDER BROTHER
grew up in Afghanistan in a humble, uneducated
family with no political connections. When the
two hardworking brothers successfully launched
a new business, extremists grew suspicious.
They assumed the young men were colluding with
Americans. Asad fled to France, and his brother
went into hiding.

I found myself on the street in Paris, with nothing and nowhere to stay. It was September, when the weather was cold, rainy, and windy, and at first I didn't have a tent or blanket. I wore the same black jeans for many days, and my feet were always wet. I was so confused. I wasn't thinking clearly.

Asad was placed in three different locations.
Each required difficult adjustments, but they also
provided life lessons, for which he is grateful.

I learned this one thing: that we are just humans, and before everything else you have to have faith and trust in humanity.

I made many friends among volunteers and aid workers. Everyone was so good. If I had a school problem, or a health problem, or even a financial problem, they were always trying to solve it for me. I trusted in their love—how much they loved refugees—but it also hurt me. It wounded me to be in a position where I needed to take these things. I questioned my dignity. I had hands, I had feet, but I couldn't work legally until my asylum was granted. I was stuck like a fly in glue.

After living for a year in refugee camps, I finally got my asylum interview, and in two months and twenty-two days, I got my answer. When I went to the post office, I was scared. My ears were warm and my feet didn't seem to work. What if the French government didn't accept me as a refugee? Then what would I do? I said to myself, "Asad, what will be your answer to your

In this photo, Asad is standing on
the place where he lived for months
in a tent after he first reached Paris.

It wounded me to be in a
position where I needed to
take these things.

I learned this one thing: that we are just humans, and before everything else you have to have faith and trust in humanity.

wife and your mother, who are waiting? And how can you begin again in a different country and learn another new language?" There were a thousand questions in my mind.

I got the post and read it, but I didn't understand it. I had Afghan friends with me, and they said, "Asad, you are safe. You are protected!" But I didn't believe it was true until I took it to my social workers, and they read it and hugged me and said, "Congratulations, Asad. You made it!" Somehow it still seemed like I was dreaming. Even now, when I wake up in the morning, my first thoughts are anxious, but then I remember and tell myself, "No, there is the envelope with your papers. You are safe."

During happy times and celebrations, my big brother comes directly into my mind. He couldn't come to Europe; he's still in hiding. And I think, "Are you happy too? Are you fine?" And I think of my wife and son—how I can get them to join me here. There is still much to worry about and work for.

ASAD, AFGHANISTAN

SABROO:

My daughter and I were Peshmerga fighters in Iraqi Kurdistan, along with my husband. In case we were arrested, we always kept one bullet to commit suicide. We fought ISIS, who are against everything. Under the name of religion they took our girls and killed our boys because they pretend they are Muslim and call us infidels. During the genocide in Shingal, ISIS raped girls, executed young boys, and buried old people alive. ISIS even raped dead bodies.

We fought against them and so sacrificed our daughter. She was killed by ISIS in 2014, while defending our country during their invasion.

SAMADI:

ISIS is not the lone enemy of the Kurdish people. Kurdistan is a country, which has territory divided among four Islamic, terrorist countries—Iraq, Iran, Syria, and Turkey. All four countries are a threat to us, then ISIS became yet another threat. The Peshmerga army is a force that puts themselves in danger to save our homeland, people, women, and children. The name Peshmerga means "those who face death." Our fight is against the fascists of Turkey, Iran, Iraq, Syria, and ISIS.

I have been a member of the Kurdistan Freedom Party for twenty-one years, since I was seventeen. I was wounded twice and jailed for four years. This party is seeking an independent Kurdistan. We fight the invading countries. We are only seeking our country's liberty; we have never tried to invade our neighboring countries' homelands. During the ISIS invasion, when we arrested fighters, we gave them food, water, and clothes, and treated them respectfully as war captives. But when they arrested us, they chained, persecuted, and treated us in inhumane ways.

After our daughter's death, we continued to face severe threats by Salafis [extreme religious groups] in Kurdistan. In order to save our family, we were obliged to leave our country.

SABROO AND SAMADI, IRAQI KURDISTAN

My daughter and I were Peshmerga
fighters in Iraqi Kurdistan, along with my
husband. In case we were arrested, we
always kept one bullet to commit suicide.

AVERY ALLEY, FRANCE

AVERY, AN AMERICAN STUDENT AT THE *American School of Paris, joined the school service club Compassion Without Borders and has spent the last two years focused on humanitarian service as well as her studies.*

My favorite activity was when we filled bags with personal toiletries and handed them out to people on the street. I think it's because we were interacting with the refugees on a one-to-one basis. I was interested to see how individuals lived in these stressful conditions. It certainly made me feel grateful for what I have on an everyday basis. I don't have to think about having enough food to eat or clothes to wear, but these people have to think about those things every day. It made me more aware of others and what their needs might be. Instead of being faceless refugees, they became people who could easily become my friends.

FOR INFORMATION ON HOW *YOU* CAN HELP, SEE PAGE 228.

NOAH READ, USA

TSOS web manager

As a younger man, I lived in Peru for two years on a mission for my church, and I came to know a different culture with many challenges that I had not faced in my own life. My first job, as I saved for college, was in a warehouse with many migrant workers. Years later, with my own family and career underway, I served in a church congregation of Spanish-speaking migrants, heard their stories, and became involved in their lives in an intimate way. The term migrant and refugee became fluid and interchangeable to me. Violence, desperate poverty, and systemic oppression pushed them all to hard lives in foreign lands.

In 2016 images of dead refugee children reached me at the same time as it appeared hearts were hardening among my countrymen. I came into contact with the founders of TSOS and knew I had to act. For things to improve for our refugee brothers and sisters, hearts need to change, and the surest way I know to change one's heart is by exercising it through exposure to the hardship, struggles, and triumphs of others. The stories of refugees give ample opportunity to exercise hearts and TSOS helps to share those stories. This is why I am involved., For things to improve for our refugee brothers and sisters, hearts need to change, and the surest way I know to change one's heart is by exercising it through exposure to the hardship, struggles, and triumphs of others.

HEATHER YOUNG, FRANCE

I WALKED INTO THE DUNKIRK CAMP IN France, and it changed my life forever. Within the first few days, I became a long-term volunteer. I have never seen anything like it. Mafia, mud, tents, children, pregnant women, disabled people, wheelchairs . . . in freezing cold, in snow, in abject misery. And yet amongst all of that, there was something . . . magic. If they have anything, they will share it with you, and more than anything they showed me a love I just haven't experienced before. It was so real, raw, soul. And they care that you care.

As volunteers, we're not giving out hope when we give out tents and sleeping bags and food. Because there isn't any. What we try to hand out is human-to-human contact. To be seen. To say, "Hey, how ya doing? You OK? You alright?" Giving your hand. Listening to them. They deserve to be heard. They just want to be able to live. You can't take them off the street necessarily . . . you can't give them asylum . . . you can't promise them anything except that you are there, you recognize their dignity as a human being.

We have a beautiful country, but something has happened to us. Our media, our government, has made us so afraid of other people. The other. Rather than embrace, we fear and we misrepresent people. We say refugee, migrant, asylum seeker, economic migrant. They are people and they are parents who fear for their children, fear for their lives, fear for their futures. There is no difference between the people you love—deeply love—and these people here. What would you do for your family? What would you do for your most cherished people? They are each cherished by someone, too. They are all people.

LINDSAY SILSBY, ENGLAND

TSOS photographer

AS THE REFUGEE CRISIS EVOLVED, I spent sleepless nights asking myself, "What if I were in the same situation? Who would help me?" I felt helpless for so long. I prayed I might be able to use my skills in a way to help these people. Months later, I had a dream about photographing refugees and telling their stories to the world. Shortly after, Their Story is Our Story: Giving Voice to Refugees (TSOS) came to fruition. I feel so grateful to have participated in this work. I pray that the viewer of my photos will see things as they really are and be moved to help these wonderful people who could be any one of us.

MY FATHER AND BROTHER
made it to Sweden; my mother and I
are trapped in Greece; my sister was
run over by a smuggler and died.
We are scattered.

NADIA, AFGHANISTAN

*Based on an interview with Nadia's
mother*

IN AFGHANISTAN, MARRIAGE IS AN AGREEMENT *between two families and not a confirmation of an emotional relationship between two individuals. Traditionally, marriage within one's own kinship group or tribe is preferred, and unions between older men and young girls are common. It is legal for men to have more than one wife.*

"Love marriages," in which couples defy their respective families' decisions on choice of spouse, are highly unusual. Those couples often face fathers and brothers who try to kill them to uphold the honor and status of the family.

My family and my wife's family didn't agree to our marriage. Her family wanted to give her to another man from their clan who was already married and had a wife. And my family wanted me to marry one of the girls in our tribe. So we went to the court and got married without our families' permission.

After we married, my wife's father and brothers found us and beat me. In the street they hit me with a car. They broke my leg and injured my jaw. They also stole my motorcycle. We went to Kabul, but during our stay there, we got a lot of phone threats. Meanwhile, Fatima got pregnant, and we decided it was time to leave the country.

We walked from Kabul to Pakistan, then to Iran. We stayed in the hot desert for four nights and five days. We drank muddy water. When we got close to Turkey, the smugglers told us the next part of our journey might be difficult because of Fatima's pregnancy, but they said it would only take about five hours. We hiked in snowy mountains and deep valleys for eighteen hours before we got to our destination, where more smugglers were waiting for us. They locked us in three rooms with forty others

After we married, my wife's father and
brothers found us and beat me. In the
street they hit me with a car. They
broke my leg and injured my jaw.

for five days until ransom money was transferred to them. Then they took us to Istanbul, then to Izmir, where they put forty-five of us in a seven-meter boat to go to Greece.

Now we're living in hot tents in a very difficult situation. My wife gave birth to our son three weeks ago, here in this camp. I talk with my mother and Fatima talks with her mother. Our mothers sigh and cry. They haven't seen how poor we are. Both of them cry.

I know I have to start and build a new life from the beginning. I hope for the day that war, prejudice, violence, corruption, and feuds between tribes are over in my country and it is safe for us to go back home.

AHMAD & FATIMA, AFGHANISTAN

THERE'S MORE TO THE STORY:
HTTPS://TSOSREFUGEES.ORG/BOOK/LINKS/1

My drawings show a time in my life when I needed love because of the sorrows along the way.

I'M FROM NIGERIA. COMING TO Italy was very difficult—very, very difficult, a real struggle. I traveled in the back of a small truck. There were many people stuck on it, maybe twenty-seven people. It was very hard to stretch your legs and be comfortable. Traveling in North Africa wasn't easy at all; it wasn't easy. The people that transport you, they don't show love.

My drawings show a time in my life when I needed love because of the sorrows along the way.

ALEX JOHNSON, NIGERIA

A Desperate Voyage Through the Sahara Desert

A Desperate Journey Through the Sea

My brother received a call saying his
son had been kidnapped. But it was not
his son; it was my son. No matter—they
slaughtered him anyway in a horribly
brutal manner. The image of his butchered
body will never leave my head.

MY BROTHER WORKED FOR THE AFGHAN NATIONAL Police in Kabul. He worked against the corruption of the powerful drug cartels, the mafia. (They are not the Taliban.) One time during a conflict, he killed one of their people, who happened to be the nephew of the mafia leader. Therefore, the mafia was always looking for revenge.

We lived with my brother. I had two sons and one daughter. My brother received a call saying his son had been kidnapped. But it was not his son; it was my son. No matter—they slaughtered him anyway in a horribly brutal manner. The image of his butchered body will never leave my head.

After that, we lived in fear. They bombed and destroyed our house two times by throwing hand grenades. One night some people shot my brother. After many days in the hospital, he recovered.

Once, I was driving to Kabul in my car when three men asked me to give them a ride and offered me good money. On the way, they suddenly attacked me. A man in the back seat put a rope around my neck and another stabbed me with a knife thirteen times—I still have the scars. They thought I was dead, so they dumped me in the snow by the road and left. Some people took me to a hospital in Kabul.

We finally decided to leave Afghanistan, but we still lived in danger. I have suffered two targeted attacks since arriving in Greece. The first one, in Lesvos, occurred following a fight I was in between Irani and Afghan people. I was put on detention, and that evening, when my wife was alone with our children, my son disappeared. He wasn't found until the middle of the next day. The second attack occurred here in Oinofyta. One night, while sleeping in our tent, we realized our tent was burning, and we went out immediately. We lost all of our belongings.

I suffer from stress and depression and headaches. We are exhausted. We simply want peace and safety for ourselves and our children.

JAMES, AFGHANISTAN

Oil on canvas, TSOS artist Elizabeth Thayer

MY HUSBAND AND I MARRIED for love, which is unusual in Afghanistan, where we lived. We are from two different ethnic groups. I am Uzbek, and James is Tajik. We fell in love, but no one in our families accepted our relationship. My family was trying to force me to marry an old man against my will, but James came secretly and we escaped to Kabul, where we got married. Because my parents did not consent, they say he kidnapped me, which brings shame on my family. For that reason, my brothers have threatened to kill James. That is one reason we fled from our country, but we still don't feel safe. My mother tells me one of my brothers is here in Greece and another is nearby in Turkey. It is still dangerous for us.

UALDA, AFGHANISTAN

STACKS OF MEMORIES

I remember my brother. He was killed and dropped at our door.

I remember when they stabbed daddy many times in the head.

I remember the first time the bombs came in our house.

I remember the other time more bombs came in our house.

I remember when Uncle opened our door and two men shot him with their guns.

I remember the cold nights in the mountains and sleeping on rocks.

I remember the night our tent burned up.

I remember . . .

KHALEEQ, AFGHANISTAN

Based on an interview with Khaleeq's father

In Syria, before we left, we were happy.
Then there was bombing and war.
Missiles and mortars were dropping.

I AM BY MYSELF WITH SIX CHILDREN. I'M exhausted with these young children on my own.

In Syria, before we left, we were happy. When we married, I was seventeen; my husband was thirty-five. It was beautiful and we were happy. Then there was bombing and war. Missiles and mortars were dropping. Four of my nephews died; they were all about the same age, twenty years old. We escaped from there to save our children.

We were smuggled by car to Turkey; then we traveled by boat to Greece, but my husband was arrested there, and he hasn't been out of jail since. I continued the journey on my own with our children.

I walked here along with everyone else who was walking until we reached here. We suffered a lot on the way. I was pregnant and had five other children. I suffered a lot. I was on my own after we left Greece. Now I don't have anyone.

My baby girl was born here in Germany. My oldest son is suffering a lot. They took him to a special school because he was causing a lot of trouble. He wants his father. My two-year-old daughter is always crying, "I want my father. I want my father." And another son has a broken leg from a bicycle accident. He also cries for his father.

I am so tired of this. I'm so tired. I am not comfortable in my life because I want my husband to come back to his children, for him to come home and raise his children. We want to bring our lives back again to the way we were before.

AISHA, SYRIA

I WAS AN AFGHAN WOMAN living in Iran. My parents fled to Iran in the late 1970's, when their little town was taken over by the Taliban. I was born in Iran. As a woman, and especially as an Afghan woman living in Iran, I had no rights, no freedom to choose my path.

My family and I had to leave everything and flee again because our lives were once again threatened by the Taliban—even in Iran. Now I am an Afghan woman living in Germany.

I only want to be treated like a human being. I just want to be free and to live in peace and safety.

SAHEBA, AFGHAN
FROM IRAN

MY NAME IS PAT. MY FATHER MARRIED THREE WIVES. HE belonged to a society that worships idols. It was a tradition in our village in West Africa. When I married, I had twins, and my father said, "This is bad juju [dark witchcraft]." He did not want to see twins; his society forbids twins. But me, as a Christian, I know that all children are good because God gives them to you.

I took my children to the pastor. For a few months, nothing happened, but then my father began looking for me. Even the village was looking for me because they wanted me to bring the children to initiate them.

They take you to a place and lay you on the ground and bring a knife and cut you. At the ceremony they sometimes kill goats, kill fowl, or kill hares, using their blood. They believe it will save you. But it will not save me. It is God that saves a person. I did not want my children to have it. I said, "No."

My husband said, "Let's leave this place and go to another village." My man was afraid. He knew people were looking for me. So we started walking to get away. Then, I don't know how they found us—maybe they used Juju [magical powers]. They found us.

They were dragging me away, and my husband said, "No, no, you can't take my wife away." They took a machete and said, "If you don't let us have this woman, we will cut you." My husband said, "No, take me, instead." But they said, "No, you are not the one we want. It is this woman and her children that are bringing problems to us because they are an abomination to us."

So they hit my husband with the machete, and he was bleeding. I tried to protect him, and they hit me with the machete, too. They took my children, and my man was dead. My heart felt dead, too.

I went to another village. There was fighting there. They were killing people because of rival tribes. After I got there, I found a woman who took me in. Her name was Blessing. I told her my name and everything that had happened to me—the reason I left my village—everything. Blessing said, "No problem, you stay with me." I lived with her for four years, but one day I was away, and when I came back, Blessing, my surrogate mother, was shot.

I decided this country would not be the end of me. I must go. I said, "This place, no longer. My life is at risk."

I went to Kano and paid money to smugglers to take me across the Sahara Desert in Libya to the seashore, where I could take a boat to Italy. In Kano, so many people were loaded into each Hilux [open-bed truck] that we almost could not breathe. Some people died. While crossing the desert, one boy died—he bled blood, bled blood and died. I was crying. I said, "God, I left my country because I don't want to die, and now people are dying in the desert."

At one place during our journey, we found water in a rock. We drank the water and ate some leaves. I saw people before me dying. I didn't want to die out there. Dead bodies because we had no water, no food to eat. We came to a wet place in the desert, and we drank the water even though there was a dead body beside it and it was smelling. We drank the water, anyway, because if we didn't we would die.

After the long journey across the desert in Libya, we finally got close to the seashore. But they didn't want us to get on boats to go to Italy. Instead a man brought a car to take a few of us to another place. But they wouldn't let us sit on the seats. He put me in the boot [trunk] but then he went away. I was in the boot for more than an hour. I was crying and shouting. I yelled, "Someone is in the boot! Someone is in the boot!" But the man was gone.

I was crying and sweating all over my body. I said, "God, make it so someone can open this boot." Immediately, God calmed me and a man came and broke the back glass. He said, "Come out." I gave thanks to God that I didn't die.

Then they took three of us to a very big place with big gates. When we went inside, a man and a woman gave the man who brought us there some money. We saw crying children and women who were pregnant. We saw more than five hundred, more than one thousand in a big hall. We slept four people in each small bed on the floor. We had to lie on our sides, back-to-stomach, to fit everyone on the bed. We could not turn. In the morning they would flog us then give us the food and a little water.

I stayed in that prison for eight months. They say it is not a prison—no police there, no uniforms—bad men run the place. Women gave birth there; they were suffering. And small, small children! I didn't cry for myself, but I cried for those children and newborn babies.

If you can bring me out of this place, I will serve you for the rest of my life. Please, show me that you are God."

There was a girl who was very small; her name was Happy. I would sometimes reserve my water for her. Once the man came and asked why she was crying. I said, "She is hungry." And he said, "She needs to be flogged." But I said, "No, flog me. Don't flog this girl because she is so small."

So the man started flogging me. See the scars? All over my body! On my arms and my back! He flogged me with iron [wire] flogs. I said, "God, I don't want to die in this prison. I left my country because I want to serve you, because I don't want to worship an idol. I don't want to die. I lost my children and my husband, and my life is at risk. That's why I left my country. If you can bring me out of this place, I will serve you for the rest of my life. Please, show me that you are God."

After one week, that man came—the man who flogged me. He said, "Come." He brought me to the gates and gave me clothes to cover me. Then he opened the gates and said, "Go! Go! Go!"

I was running, running and fell into a hole. It was deep. I stood up to catch my breath. Then I ran again and found a place to hide, because if anyone saw me they would take me back to the prison. Someone did find me. His name was Pork. He said, "What are you doing here?" And when he saw my body, he began to cry. I was crying, also. He took me to his house and I told him my story. He said he could not hide me there, but he would help me.

Soon his brother came and took me to the sea. They put me in a boat with other people. I thought I would die in the sea, but God saved me. I was rescued and fainted. They took me to a hospital in Sicily, and I was there for three days. They gave me some treatments for my wounds. Then they took me to this place [a refugee camp in Italy]. It is eight months since I came to this country.

When I told my story to a lady here, she said, "Pat, your life is saved."

PAT, WEST AFRICA

They would have forcibly married my girls off.

I HAVE SIX CHILDREN, FOUR DAUGHTERS and two sons. My husband was a soldier. He lost both of his feet when he was fighting to defend our homeland. He died four years ago because his feet kept pouring out filth.

After he was injured, my daughters and I were in danger because we had no man to speak for us or to protect us. Everybody protested and told us, "Your husband is a cripple, and he cannot protect his wife and children." After his death, our situation became even worse. They said my daughters must get married. But my daughters refused. They would have forcibly married my girls off and their studies would have been in vain. They would have destroyed their lives, and it would be worse for me.

I brought my daughters here for their sake. I told them that regardless of what happens to me, they must be in a safe place, for they have their own wishes, too.

Faribah and five of her children are currently living destitute in a camp in Serbia, trapped behind closed borders and cut off from opportunity. They are unable to go back, and unable to move ahead.

FARIBAH, AFGHANISTAN

I MARRIED WHEN I WAS ten-years-old. My husband was Iranian; I am from Afghanistan. We were married for 40 years and didn't have any children. After he died, his family didn't want me because I am from Afghanistan. I wasn't allowed to stay in my house or get money from the bank. Now I am alone, living in a tent here in Greece.

BAHAR, AFGHANISTAN

One time, I was singing at a wedding
party when the local Taliban attacked
me with shovels and hoes and rocks
because I was performing for the
women's part in a wedding.

I WAS A SINGER. WE LEFT BECAUSE THE Taliban and ISIS do not like music or musicians.

I worked in the Baghlan district for a radio program called Sana Radio and as a singer for official events and ceremonies. One time, I was singing at a wedding party when the local Taliban attacked me with shovels and hoes and rocks because I was performing for the women's part in a wedding. They said, "Why is there a male singer with the women? Why?"

After that, I decided to move to the city of Kabul, but, as everyone knows, it is always dangerous there with suicide bombings and the Taliban. Again, my life was threatened in Kabul. The Taliban threw a letter with their threats into my home. I still have that letter. Another time, at about 2 a.m., two men attacked me when I was coming out of a restaurant. I ran to my motorcycle and escaped.

We had a good life there— my wife, my children, and I. We had a house, a car, and a good income. I had to sell everything and leave the country to save our lives. I left behind my mother and brothers and sisters.

MOHAMMAD AZAM AND
SONS, FARZAD AND SUHAIL,
AFGHANISTAN

SARAH KIPPEN WOOD, USA

TSOS data coordinator

MY GRANDMOTHER WAS A MASTER AT crossword puzzles, with a quick wit and an easy laugh. She was also a refugee. Famine and ethnic persecution prompted my grandmother's Volga German family to escape from Russia in 1921. My great-grandfather paid a million rubles for false passports when my grandmother was a young toddler. While trying to flee, their train broke down, and Nana's father carried her across the border into Poland, where the young family was captured and incarcerated. After some months in dire conditions, a German farmer and his church helped them get out of detention and into the Frankfurt area of Germany. In Frankfurt, my great-grandfather worked, put together immigration papers, and found sponsorship to move to the US.

Since my grandmother passed away over ten years ago, I have felt a growing sense of urgency to help today's refugees; that desire led me to seek out volunteer work with TSOS. In October 2017, I had the opportunity to travel with TSOS to Frankfurt to help with a new round of refugee interviews. Perhaps not coincidentally, that trip took me to the very soil where my own family sought and obtained refuge nearly a century ago.

For my grandmother, once her family reached Germany there was a clear path forward to begin a new life. For many of the people TSOS has interviewed, there is no clear path forward.

In today's refugee children, I see my grandmother. I see in their eyes the rich legacies they will pass on to their families and communities—if they are given a chance to do so. At this moment, they need us. And we need them.

MARJORIE BURT, USA

MY NAME IS MARJORIE BURT. I WAS A service missionary for The Church of Jesus Christ of Latter-day Saints in Germany. I went two days a week to refugee camps to work with the children. First of all, we would bring hugs and smiles. And secondly, we brought activities—things like games, playing jump rope, teaching them how to write on the pavement with chalk. Teaching them a few German words, since we knew they would be required to learn the language.

We were received with great affection and love. We were all struggling with language, but what I learned right away was heart to heart communication. We didn't have to speak the same language, but we all understood each other. It was special to me to relate as mother to mother, friend to friend, child to grown up. I felt like all the children were my substitute grandchildren while I was in Germany.

To anyone who gets a spark of inspiration, a desire to help these special people, I would say, "Just do it! Give it your whole heart and doors will open and understanding will grow."

The Brown Family, Germany

I'M KIMBALL BROWN, FROM IDAHO IN the USA, and my wife, Valentina, is from Bulgaria. We live in Germany with our three children in an American military community. People here are always moving in and out, and sometimes they leave things behind, like bicycles. In 2016, Val read an article about people in refugee camps and the troubles they have with transportation. We thought, "We need to give these abandoned bikes to refugees."

Once the word got out, people began donating more bikes. We bought some oil, and I put the kids to work fixing flat tires and cleaning rusty chains. When the bikes were done, I loaded them onto my car and delivered them to the camp in Rebstock. After a while, the camp even set up a bike repair shop. Refugees with mechanical skills work there. It fills a need to be able to do something meaningful.

A lot of the bikes we get are kids' bikes. Probably the most touching experience I've had with this project was watching a dad teach his daughter how to ride a bike. I thought, "That's what life is about. If we can give a parent an opportunity to have this bonding experience with their kid, then it was so worth it to us and such a blessing."

When I look at the diversity I see in Germany now, I don't think it's something to be feared. We need to get away from the *them* and *us* mentality. Most refugees are people of goodwill, and that's what we need. The world has enough problems naturally; we don't need to waste time fighting.

The refugee crisis is a legitimate crisis, but it's also an opportunity for us to say, "We're your friends, so let's break down the walls." There are walls everywhere that need to be broken down.

Kathryn M. Cunningham, USA

TSOS writer

I STARTED WRITING SHORT STORIES when my husband was in graduate school and I was struggling to manage our limited finances, take care of our four children, and work through my growing depression. Writing allowed me to find peace in my pain. Now, writing real life refugees' stories helps me to honor my refugee friends from the past, shine a light on those who need our help today, and assist in making our world a safer, friendlier home for all in the future.

FOR INFORMATION ON HOW YOU CAN HELP, SEE PAGE 228.

Now that we have left, we can never go back. My husband would be jailed and tortured.

WE ARE QASHQAI TURKS, SHIA MUSLIMS, from southern Iran. My husband and I were very sad to leave our homeland because our families have been there for many generations. It was a difficult decision, but the future of our children is very important to us. We have two children, and soon we will have three. But the government of Iran discriminates against us. We had no support from the government. My husband was not allowed to study at a university, to obtain a job, or to own a home because of our ethnicity. We are a minority group, and we don't have the right to protest. Some brave people we know protested, and they disappeared or were hanged. This made us decide to leave. Now that we have left, we can never go back. My husband would be jailed and tortured.

We must think about the future of our children.

NASIRA, IRAN

I have never known peace.

WE HAVE HAD WAR IN
Afghanistan since before I was
born—bombings, explosions,
the Taliban, insecurity, corruption. I have never known peace.
I don't want my child to have
the trouble I've had. I want him
to grow up in peace.

HENNA, AFGHANISTAN

I want to be a hairdresser, because I learned how to do it in my hometown.

MY NAME IS HANIAH. LIFE IN MY home country in West Africa is not bad, but you cannot get good work. My boyfriend left because of that problem, because of the work. We didn't have money. So he left me with two babies and went to Libya. I didn't hear from him at all—I got no information. I decided to go to look for him. I left the two babies with my mom and went to Libya, but I didn't find him.

I found somebody to help me come to Italy in a ship. It was not easy. Some of the people died. God helped me with everything. When I came to Italy, and I found my boyfriend, he told me he wanted to marry me. I got pregnant. My boyfriend told me to come to this city. I took the train to come here. I gave birth, and they transferred me to this women's shelter with my baby, Hope. My boyfriend comes to visit us.

I want to be a hairdresser, because I learned how to do it in my hometown. I know how to do braids. I want Hope to go to school. I fast and I pray to God. God knows what I am, so He will help me. He helped me come here. He helped me to do what I needed to do.

HANIAH, WEST AFRICA

Charcoal drawing, TSOS artist Elizabeth Thayer

All the time in my dreams I see my family drowning in the sea. I don't want to ever go back to the sea!

MY NAME IS ZARRIN. I WAS AN ENGLISH TEACHER. IN Afghanistan I had a big house and a garden. My husband was a rich man; he had lots of money. My children studied in a private school.

All the time, the Taliban was warning my husband, "Why does your wife go to school and teach children? If your wife goes to school, we'll throw acid on her face and take your children." They don't like education—they don't like women attending school.

After receiving numerous death threats from the Taliban, Zarrin and her husband fled their home and endured an arduous journey from Afghanistan through Iran and into Turkey. There she faced her greatest fear—the sea crossing between Turkey and Greece.

I went to the ship despairing. When we got into the boat, lots of water was coming in—my clothes, my children—I was afraid my children would die in the sea. The sea was stormy! Very rough! My husband had gathered all of our money into a backpack, and the backpack was with me in the back [of the boat]. The mafia said to me, "All in the back, take and throw your things into the sea. If you do not throw everything into the sea, maybe you will all drown." The ship was full of water. Water! I was so distressed I didn't remember our money was in the backpack. The Mafia took all things in the back [of the boat] and threw them into the sea.

When we arrived on the island, Greece, my husband called me. "Where is your bag?" I said, "In the sea." When my husband saw my bag was not in the boat, he began shouting and fell out onto the ground. The doctor came and examined my husband— he checked him and after that they brought an ambulance and gave oxygen because he didn't have breath. Because of the money. Now we have none.

All the time in my dreams I see my family drowning in the sea. I don't want to ever go back to the sea!

ZARRIN, AFGHANISTAN

Because I was pregnant, they allowed me and my children to continue to the mainland, but they kept my husband in the camp on the island.

MY NAME IS MORENA. I AM PREGNANT and have two children with my husband. In Afghanistan, my husband was a truck driver. He carried fuel and gas while working for an American company. During the night, the Taliban appeared in front of his truck and took it. They were about to attack him when he escaped. We felt we were all in danger, so we came here. There were problems on the way. We had so many problems.

We finally arrived in Greece on a ship, but then we were separated. Because I was pregnant, they allowed me and my children to continue to the mainland, but they kept my husband in the camp on the island. It is not acceptable to separate a husband and wife, but it happened. This is what the Greek police did to us.

After my husband and I became separated, I stayed in a park with my two young children for two weeks. I was thinking of suicide. What other decision could there be? I was so tired of life. My brother found me and brought us to this camp. I was very tired.

My husband is still in the camp on the island, and we are still separated. They won't allow him to come here, and I don't want to go there because the conditions are terrible in the camp, and my doctor says I should stay here for the safety of my unborn baby. I am a lonely woman with two children.

MORENA, AFGHANISTAN

Oil on canvas, TSOS artist Elizabeth Thayer

WE WERE CROSSING THE BORDER
when the police came and split our group in two.
Our three-year-old boy was lost on the other side
of the border. He was gone for two days before
we could pay a smuggler to get him back to us.
It was all the money we had; we were so afraid.

ZARGHONA AND MEHRULLAH,
AFGHANISTAN

It was snowing. It was so very hard. We did not even hope to see the light of day.

MY HUSBAND'S FATHER WAS A PUBLIC figure. He held a high position in the Afghan state. He was attacked, beaten, and forced to leave his job. Now one of his hands and his feet are paralyzed. Now he cannot walk at all.

We had to leave. We had many problems. We called a smuggler. They treated us with hate. No sleep at night, no food for days. Turkish police caught and beat my husband. We couldn't understand what they were saying, but they beat him and punished him. We spent several nights in the mountains without water or bread. It was snowing. It was so very hard. We did not even hope to see the light of day.

Zarghona gave birth to a healthy baby just days after sharing her story with us. After spending more than nine months in Greece, she and her husband decided to once again pay a smuggler to guide them and their four children across the closed borders and up into Serbia—a distance of 470 miles. Since leaving their homeland in 2016, they have traveled over 3000 miles across six countries, and are still without a home.

ZARGHONA, AFGHANISTAN

THERE'S MORE TO THE STORY:
HTTPS://TSOSREFUGEES.ORG/BOOK/LINKS/7

Our children are here for hope—a hope to be educated, a hope to be free, and a hope to be away from wars.

WE ARE FROM THE HAZARA PROVINCE OF DAYKUNDI IN CENTRAL Afghanistan. We are Shiite. When the Taliban came to our town, they took many of the men and beheaded them. They enslaved women and kidnapped children. We didn't dare leave our house. Under no condition! We didn't dare step out. We lived secretly. We finally fled.

There were twenty of us traveling together. While at the Iran-Turkey border, we crossed a river at night. The water was deep, and it was raining. Then the Turkish patrol caught us. They kept us out in the cold until morning. All of our clothes were wet, but still they kept us unsheltered in the freezing rain. In the morning, they sent us back to the border again. . . . To hide, we went into the tall reeds in the lake and sat in water up to our waists all day long until late at night, until midnight.

Finally, the smuggler who had brought us there came to us in the middle of the second night and gave us a phone. He said to listen to the person on the phone, and we would be guided. Then he left us. We listened to the man on the phone giving us directions. We got to a river and crossed it, then to a second river, which was much deeper. I had my youngest child tied around my waist.

The taller men crossed first to see how deep it was, then they came back and carried the children in their arms. Then they returned and took women's hands to help them across. This was at about three or four o'clock in the morning.

After we crossed, we then had to climb hills. It was raining and slippery. Everyone had difficulty climbing. We took one of our scarves and pulled people up by letting them hold on. We finally came to a road, where the traffickers waited in a van. Patrols were coming, so the traffickers began to panic and were going to leave some of us behind because there wasn't enough room, but we begged, and finally they threw us inside, closed the door, and went.

We drove for two or three hours. They took us to a barn filled with mud. It smelled. All of us were soaking wet. The children had fevers. Farooz's was very high. They hadn't had food or water for two days and nights. Parisa's lips were bloody and stuck. I realized I was losing my children.

I went to the man working there. I begged him [to help], saying my child was about to die. I told him my children had had nothing in two days, not even a drop of water. He asked me why this was so, and I told him, "Because of your colleagues, the traffickers!"

When he looked into their faces, he felt pity. He used a piece of a warm, wet cloth to make Parisa's lips wet and gently separated them. Then he gave her water to drink. My children had trouble swallowing water in their mouths. Then he gave us a few pistachio nuts. After two or three hours, they began talking again. But two of my children still had fevers.

My son, Farooz, who was so sick during those cold nights, has never gotten completely well. He had a sore throat and swollen tonsils. And he now stutters.

Our children are here for hope—a hope to be educated, a hope to be free, and a hope to be away from wars.

Not long after we interviewed Linar, her husband was killed during an argument with a smuggler. The rest of the family have received asylum in Greece, are settled into a home, and the children are finally attending school.

LINAR, AFGHANISTAN

Economically, we had everything but my daughter was poisoned at her school, and my son's school was bombed.

I OWNED A DRUGSTORE. BEFORE that, I worked for a US mine-clearing institute for fifteen years. Economically, we had everything but my daughter was poisoned at her school, and my son's school was bombed. We received threats several times, and I was forced to close my store.

We just want peace. We want to be free from fear and panic. My children want to go to school. We want to be somewhere that is far from danger, somewhere safe.

SALMAN, AFGHANISTAN

Etching, Nathaneal Read

They hit my grandmother.

WE DEFIED THE TALIBAN. THEY found me because I hadn't gone into hiding with the rest of my family. I lived with our one-hundred-year-old grandmother and took care of her. They knew where we lived, so they came. They hit my grandmother. They beat me with iron rods and asked where my family was hiding. I wouldn't tell them, and I tried to run away. They ran me over with their car and left me for dead.

Neighbors took me to the hospital. I was in a coma. It took my family three days to find me.

Now we are in Germany. I have scars all over my body. I have seizures. The worst part, though, is the nightmares. I can't sleep.

I love to play soccer. I love to work and cook. I forget things a lot, and I can't read. I really love soccer.

EDREES, AFGHAN FROM IRAN

The Taliban kidnapped my eight-year-old sister in front of our house.

WE HAD A GOOD LIFE—A HOUSE and a car and a good income. My father used to work on trains in Herat before the Taliban threatened to kill us. The Taliban kidnapped my eight-year-old sister in front of our house. She passed away from her injuries two weeks before we left the country. We didn't have hope, and we decided to leave. I don't believe that our country will ever be a safe place to live. The Taliban is still there. We can't go back.

ORZALA, AFGHANISTAN

I HAD A GOOD LIFE IN Afghanistan; I had a mechanic shop. Where we worked and lived there are two groups of Taliban militants. Both of them claim power and influence in the area, and they have armed conflicts with each other. One group of militants called me to fix their vehicle. I went to fix it, but the other group of militants arrested me and threatened me for fixing the vehicle of the opposing group.

Our lives were in danger no matter what we did. If we worked for either of the Taliban groups, the government would arrest us; but if we worked for the government, the Taliban would arrest us.

Taliban militants killed two of my neighbors in the mechanic shop where I worked. They also killed my cousin, also a mechanic. That's why we left.

Twenty of us traveled together. We went to Iran, then Turkey, then Bulgaria. We were captured in Bulgaria and spent three nights in the forest. In Bulgaria the police beat me and took all my possessions. We were returned to Turkey, then from Turkey we came to Greece by the sea. I am here with my wife and one-year-old daughter.

By the time Habib and his family finally made it to Greece, they had nothing left but each other. The camp near Athens where they lived temporarily was a place of temperature extremes, ranging from over 100 degrees in the summer to below freezing and snowy in winter. Rows upon rows of tents were all that stood in defense of either extreme. Yet the community offered relative safety. The refugees worked together to cook, clean, sort donations, play soccer, create art, and meet together to peacefully resolve disputes. The camp closed in December 2017, and the refugees were once again displaced. Currently, Habib's location and that of his family are unknown.

HABIB, AFGHANISTAN

I'd like to be a famous chemist in the future.

DANIAL FLED WITH HIS MOTHER AND THREE of *his siblings on foot from Kabul to Germany in 2015. They were kidnapped by thugs preying on refugees at the border between Afghanistan and Iran and held for ransom. His oldest sister, who had stayed in Kabul because of the dangers which await young women on the borders, had to quickly sell everything they owned within three days to pay the ransom. In captivity, a motorcycle fell on his little sister and broke her foot. Their captors refused to treat it. Finally the money was sent, they were released, and his sister's foot was treated. His older sister flew to Tehran, and together they continued the three-thousand-mile journey to Frankfurt, Germany, where they now live. Danial and his family are safe, learning German, and appreciating the freedom and security they never knew in Afghanistan.*

I like chemistry so much! I'd like to be a famous chemist in the future. My parents brought me here despite all the problems and difficulties so I could have a future. I want to be a useful person and follow my dreams. I'm sure I will do that. From now on, I have to do my best.

DANIAL, AFGHANISTAN

Oil on canvas, TSOS artist Elizabeth Benson Thayer

A MESSAGE TO
THE WORLD

"The world is indeed full of peril, and in it there are many dark places; but still there is much that is fair, and though in all lands love is now mingled with grief, it grows perhaps the greater."

—J.R.R. TOLKIEN, *THE FELLOWSHIP OF THE RING*

ARTIST ELIZABETH THAYER:

THERE ARE CURRENTLY 22.5 MILLION REFUGEES IN THE WORLD. Over half of them are children; hundreds of thousands of them are children traveling alone. They have fled violence, conflict, and intense persecution in the hope that the rest of the world will show some humanity.

Children are the first to see magic, the last to lose hope. Long after adults have given in to despair and cynicism, a child believes in that which is good and right. That is why in the middle of a dusty, abandoned factory-turned-refugee-camp in Greece, you can still hear laughs and cries, hear the patter of feet on the cement floor, and feel a tiny hand slip into yours. Despite all that has happened in their short lives, they are willing to trust, to make a new friend, to hope for love returned.

These three boys fled violence and persecution in Afghanistan, undertook perilous journeys with their families, and landed in the refugee camp in Greece where I met them. One of them trailed me all day, wanting to play, laugh, hold hands, and watch me draw. The others scuffled in the dirt, took turns on the one bicycle in the camp, bossed the younger children, annoyed the teenage girls, struck endless 'peace' and 'love' poses for the camera, and generally got underfoot, all with the youthful optimism of a Cub Scout.

Their future is uncertain, and their past is gone forever. This precarious position could understandably inspire fear, mistrust, and despair. Yet so often it is the children who are able to rise above the rhetoric of fear and show us all what humanity really means.

APPENDIX

FLEEING

CONSIDER WHAT IT WOULD BE LIKE TO wake up one morning and find your neighborhood under attack by a vicious, radicalized militia on the ground or indiscriminate bombing from above. Normal routines—work, school, social life—would come to an abrupt halt. Safety for yourself and your family would become your highest priority. Firoz, a fourteen year old boy, experienced this firsthand:

In Syria, our lives were full of happiness. All our relatives were together. . . . Our village was quiet even though it was full of people. . . . ISIS invaded our village on the first day of the revolution. They began killing people without mercy because we don't share their religion. . . . They kept killing—they killed so many. They didn't bury them; they threw them in pits. . . . Our whole lives are destroyed.

People with normal lives, people just like you and me, continue to be ripped from their comfortable homes and associations when war comes to their doorstep. Ahktar, who owned five thriving businesses, lost everything but his life:

Let me tell you something: I never in my life thought to leave Syria. Our lives there were far better than now. We were living with family and with our people. But then came the constant shooting and bombs. Then came the siege and hunger. . . . You don't know when you might die. . . . They are destroying the country until there is nothing left. It's a tragedy, a tragedy. One day you're living like a king, then suddenly you find yourself at the bottom. So we left. We had no choice.

Zarrin, from Afghanistan, also found her world turned unexpectedly upside down:

My husband was a rich man. . . . My children studied in a private school. My house was three stories tall, with four rooms on each floor. My home was cool with air conditioning. We had a big hall—very big—with six carpets. I had a beautiful garden. When I went to school to teach, I had servants working for me. When I came home, my food was ready and my house was clean. Now, when I remember my house, I cry. I don't have any money. Here in the camp, women gather to talk together in a tent—sometimes crying, sometimes laughing as we remember.

Dr. Abdul Nasser Kaadan, of Aleppo, Syria, is a highly regarded physician and scholar. He has been an orthopedic surgeon since 1986, is the founder and president of the International Society for the History of Islamic Medicine, and was a professor and department chair at Aleppo University. He has participated in more than one hundred international conferences outside Syria, has four-dozen published papers and six books, and was nominated for a Nobel Prize in literature in 2012. But his honors, credentials, and vital work could not keep him safe in his home country. Dr. Kaadan and his wife, Roua Hajjar, left war-torn Syria when they realized their lives were in danger. He explained:

*Dr. Abdul
Nasser
Kaadan*

I was living near Aleppo University, which was under the government's control. I left in early 2015 when the situation became very dangerous. There were bombings every day and attacks on civilians. One of my colleagues at Aleppo University was killed in a bomb attack while he was in his car with his son; they both died. Another colleague, a surgeon, was arrested by the government and tortured until he died for giving medical treatment to an injured patient who happened to be a member of the opposition. This is what my family and I faced every day. I left my private hospital, my private clinic,

my cars—I left everything behind, and some of them are destroyed now. But I'm not thinking about what I lost; I'm sad, but I'm also happy because I have good health and a good mind and we are safe. If I have those three things, money is nothing at all.

BORDERS

THE EUROPEAN REFUGEE CRISIS BEGAN in 2015, when rising numbers of people fleeing war and violence in Middle Eastern countries arrived in the European Union (EU) by traveling in boats over the Aegean Sea or walking overland through southeast Europe. The scope of the migration is staggering. EU countries struggling to cope with the crisis have funded increased border patrol operations and constructed physical barriers (mostly razor-wire fences) in efforts to discourage the entry of refugees. However, desperate people take desperate measures in order to reach countries where they hope to settle their families in a safe environment. Border crossings make their journeys more difficult and dangerous, but when what lies behind is worse than what lies ahead, refugees take the risks.

Linar, the mother of four young children, described an extraordinary experience of being caught between two borders:

There were twenty of us traveling together. While at the Iran-Turkey border, we crossed a river at night. The water was deep, and it was raining. Then the Turkish patrol caught us. They kept us out in the cold until morning. All of our clothes were wet, but still they kept us unsheltered in the freezing rain. In the morning, they sent us back to the border again. We were at a lake. The Turkish border guard was hitting us, even our children, to make us cross the water. We were crying and screaming, telling him we would drown there—the children would drown. He pushed an old woman into the water. Young men rescued her. We screamed and cried so much the Turkish guard finally quit pushing us and left us there alone.

Linar: "My son, Farooz, who was so sick during those cold nights, has never gotten completely well."

Then Iranian patrols came. They pointed guns at us and told us to return the way we came, which meant back to Turkey. We were stuck between two patrols. Both sides were firing guns. They wouldn't allow us to move either way; neither side wanted us in their country. We were completely stuck. To hide, we went into the tall reeds in the lake and sat in water up to our waists all day long until late at night, until midnight. And it was still raining. We had no food, no good water, nothing. My son, Farooz, was burning up with fever. I thought he would die. Finally, the smuggler who had brought us there came to us in the middle of the second night and showed us the way to escape.

Ali, at the Juares Metro Station in Paris, where he and countless refugees lived for months in tents.

Border crossings became monumental challenges for Bilal and Ali, two young Afghan men who became best friends after they met each other in a refugee camp in Greece. Bilal was determined to make it to central Europe. He tried and repeatedly failed:

> I've already tried ten times to cross the border into Macedonia or Bulgaria, but each time I've been caught by the Greek police, the Serbian police, or the Bulgarian police. Once I hid on a train I thought was going from Greece to Germany, but the train didn't go to Germany. It went instead to a manufacturing company in Greece. The Greek police opened the boxcar door and said with big grins, "Welcome to Germany." If I have to try forty more times, I will not stop until I get out of Greece.

Tragically, shortly after his interview with TSOS, Bilal drowned while swimming in the sea nearby. His devastated friend Ali immediately left to make his own desperate escape to Europe:

> I left Greece. I couldn't stay. But the European borders were closed. Bulgaria was closed. Everything from Greece was closed. I hid under a truck a semitrailer truck when the driver was off his shift. I lay underneath on top of a cross beam and waited for five or six hours before he came back. He didn't see me. Then the truck began moving. I lay under it for thirty-six hours—no food, little water. It was very, very dangerous. I kept thinking, "I will be dead; I'm not going to make it."

But Ali did make it—all the way to France, arriving with nothing. He joined thousands of other refugees who slept under bridges on the sidewalks of Paris, with only his light jacket and the steam rising from a manhole to keep him warm. Since arriving there, he has made new friends who have helped him in his bid to seek asylum in France.

SMUGGLERS

IN REFUGEE TERMS, *SMUGGLING* GEN-
erally refers to one person paying another to sneak
him or her across borders past armed guards.

Refugees normally pay smugglers hundreds
and sometimes thousands of euros per person in
order to get into countries with closed borders. The
tighter the security, the higher the risk, the higher
the price. With today's closed borders causing the
intense flow of human traffic to go underground,
smuggling is a billion-dollar business.

Refugees rely on local smugglers to guide them
in areas they know nothing about. It's worth it to
them to pay the price. Ahmad and his pregnant wife,
Fatima, walked hundreds of miles from Afghanistan
to Greece and dealt with multiple smugglers:

> We walked from Kabul to Pakistan, then
> to Iran, with smugglers helping us at the
> borders. We stayed in the hot desert for
> four nights and five days. . . . When we got
> close to Turkey, the smugglers told us the
> next part of our journey might be difficult
> because of Fatima's pregnancy, but they
> said it would only take about five hours.
> We hiked in snowy mountains and deep
> valleys for eighteen hours before we got to
> our destination, where more smugglers were
> waiting for us. They locked us in three rooms
> with forty others for five days until ransom
> money was transferred to them.

Holding refugees for ransom is not uncommon
in the smuggling business, which is illegal from
the start. Many smugglers prey upon vulnerable
refugees by extorting money from family members
back home, as in this case described by Roksana, a
young Afghan woman:

> My mother and siblings had a very difficult
> time on their way to Iran. Every day I was

thinking about where they were and what
might be happening to them. One day my
mother called me and asked me to send
money. She didn't tell me they were being
held for ransom by smugglers because she
knew I would be very worried. But I figured
out what was happening to them. I had to
sell things in our house quickly. Within
two or three days I collected about twenty
million tomans [Iranian currency equaling
nearly $5300]. I sent the money, and when
my mother called me again and told me they
were free, I was very happy.

One refugee described smugglers as "not
human at all," saying, "They simply make a lot of
money and put us at great risk." Another refugee's
story illustrates this lack of humanity. "We came by
sea," she said, "and the smugglers abandoned us on
a deserted island. We took off our life jackets and set
them on fire to get warm. My children suffered with
me. They were exhausted. . . . We begged passing
fishermen to rescue us. When we paid them money,
they took us off the island."

In a similar instance, a different smuggler also
abandoned his clients—this time in the mountains
of Iran. One of the men in the group told his story:

> I hired smugglers and travelled for many
> days, through Iran and Turkey and into
> Greece. The other refugees and I were
> packed into taxis, trucks, and the trunks of
> smugglers' cars, always barely escaping the
> police. We never had enough to eat, nor clean
> drinking water. When we stopped for the
> night, we couldn't sleep because there were
> so many people and it was so cold. When we
> came to the mountains, we had to continue
> our trip on foot through the snow. We had to
> hide from the army, and in the middle of the

A refugee family warms themselves during one of their multiple border crossing attempts.

With the help of smugglers, refugees in Hungary go through a razor-wire fence at the Serbian border.

journey, the smuggler just pointed the way we should go and left us in the mountains alone.

Already traumatized by events that caused them to leave their home countries, desperate individuals and families fleeing violence often suffer again at the hands of unethical smugglers. Some pay the ultimate price when dealing with them. One refugee died after being knifed by a smuggler while arguing over money. In another case, an Afghan refugee grieved over his family's loss at the hands of negligent smuggler. His story: "In Iran, another smuggler vehicle arrived. The car stopped so we could get in. Just as I stepped into the car to sit down, it moved onward. Half of my body was still not inside the car, and it drove over my sister's young daughter. She died. The image is still in front of my eyes."

LIBYA

SUB-SAHARAN AFRICAN REFUGEES IN transit towards European countries usually travel through Libya before crossing the Mediterranean Sea to Italy and points beyond. Since the fall of Muammar Gaddafi in 2011, Libya has become a breeding ground for gangs who kidnap, enslave, and extort money from refugees and migrants. Many of these vulnerable people suffer some of the most extreme experiences of our time.

People smugglers force their human cargo into overcrowded trucks for treacherous journeys across the Sahara. One refugee from Nigeria said:

Libya, it was hell. To cross the desert, we were about twenty-four in the truck. Some Arabs on motorcycles jumped us in the middle of the night and started shooting. Eight of our people died. For about two days we were in the desert. We had no place to hide. We were drinking our own urine. Only six of us came out alive.

One refugee was horrified by the lawless and rampantly violent world he met in Libya. He observed:

An excellent source for learning more about those traveling migratory routes through Libya is EXODI, "an interactive web map built using the testimonies of 2,600 migrants from Sub-Saharan Africa collected over four years of activity (2014–2017) by the operators and volunteers of Medici per i Dirritti Umani/Doctors for Human Rights (MEDU)." Information MEDU gleans from their extensive interviews reaffirms what TSOS learned from our own story collecting. The following is from the MEDU website:

Torture, Inhuman and Degrading Treatments

About 90% of surveyed migrants said they had been victims of extreme violence, torture and inhuman and degrading treatment in the country of origin and/or along the migration route, particularly in detention and abduction places in Libya. Deprivation of food and water, poor hygienic condition, frequent beatings and other forms of blunt trauma are the most common and widespread forms of ill-treatment. In addition, migrants report the following types of violence: beatings to the feet (falaka); torture for suspension and stress positions (handcuffing, standing position for an extended time, etc.); burnings; threats to them, or to their families; rapes and sexual outrages; religious insults and other forms of degrading treatment; deprivation of medical care. In most of the cases, migrants were forced to witness other people subjected to torture and cruelty. Nine out of ten migrants said they had seen someone die, be killed, tortured or severely beaten.

"It was like I was in a movie. But at the end of the day, it wasn't playful. I worried about how my life would end. When we got there, military gangs searched us for everything we had. They took it all. They don't work; they just want to get money or other things. If you are a girl traveling along the roadside, they will want you to sleep with them or give them something, or you won't be able to pass. Fifteen-year-old boys had guns, and they drove good cars. If you touched them, or looked at them, or said something they didn't like, they would shoot you. The humans there are like animals."

After crossing the desert, competing militias force refugees into detention centers where thousands of men, women, and children are imprisoned in grim, unsanitary, overcrowded conditions, deprived of food and abused by their captors. They are treated as slave labor until they pay off what they owe to the illegal human traffickers. One woman survived eight months of brutal treatment in a Libyan prison. She described the conditions and the "bad men who ran the place:"

They took three of us to a very big place with big gates. When we went inside, a man and a woman gave the man who brought us there

some money. We saw crying children and women who were pregnant. We saw more than five hundred, more than one thousand in a big hall. We slept four people in each small bed on the floor. We had to lie on our sides, back to stomach, to fit everyone on the bed. We could not turn. In the morning they would flog us and then give us food and a little water. . . . Women gave birth there; they were suffering. And small, small children! I didn't cry for myself, but I cried for those children and newborn babies.

These young African refugees (photographed here in Naples) traveled through the living hell called Libya while attempting to reach European shores. Each one has a horrific, personal story to tell. They are representative of tens of thousands more who face kidnapping, slavery, torture, extortion, and sexual violence in Libya before crossing the Mediterranean Sea to Italy—if they are not killed first. The risks, which are well known, are a stark gauge of how desperate African refugees and migrants are in their search for safety and better opportunities in Europe.

SEAS

AFRICAN REFUGEES WHO HAVE FLED wars at home and survived Libya's treacheries might think the worst of their journey is behind them, but when they get to the Libyan coastline, they face the almost unutterable horror of being forced into unseaworthy boats to cross the vast, unforgiving Mediterranean. Thousands never arrive at their destination.

"I spent nine months in Libya calling my parents every month to get more money," reported a refugee from Nigeria. "My mom sent me 100,000 euro, and I had to give it to the man. . . . We pushed out five boats; four capsized during the journey. A lot of souls died in that sea. There were people calling for their children—their son, their daughter. The others would lie, 'They aren't here; we do not have them. They are not dead.' For so long they were calling. Hoping. Not knowing they had died."

A father from Sierra Leone, who was attempting to escort his seven-year-old daughter to freedom, said, "They forced us to get into the sea and shot two people in front of me who didn't want to get in the boat. I didn't have any option. When the boat started going out to sea, my daughter cried. I cried. My daughter vomited in the boat. We were eleven hours in the sea, then a big ship came and rescued us. They took us to Italy."

In 2016, a record 181,000 migrants crossed between Libya and Italy. More than 4,500 are known to have died. In an attempt to restrict the flow of refugees into southern Europe, some European states are actively supporting the Libyan Coast Guard with

Refugees on the Aegean Sea between Turkey and Greece.

with markings that alert the coast guard to let them pass through Libyan waters without interception.

The other major sea crossing—between Turkey and Greece—has also claimed thousands of lives due to crisis crossings. When asked about their journeys, most land-bound refugees consider the sea their biggest horror. "We all knew that if we got on this boat, we could die," a young father told us. "But we didn't have another option. So we paid for our death. You cannot imagine how dangerous it was in that boat! All the way I kept praying for my family. And I imagined what I would do if the boat collapsed. How many people could I save? . . . I probably couldn't even save my own daughter, my own wife."

Like this father, a mother with a family of young children emphatically declared:

"I don't want to ever go back to the sea! All the time in my dreams I see my family drowning. I went to the ship despairing, When we got into the boat, lots of water was coming in—my clothes, my children—I was afraid my children would die in the sea. The sea was stormy! Very rough! The waves were coming into the boat, but we could see the border police were coming. My husband saw them and shouted that he didn't want to stay in Turkey, so we stayed in the boat despite the danger. My husband had gathered all of our money into a backpack, and the backpack was with me in the back [of the boat]. The mafia said to us, "All in the back, take and throw your things into the sea. If you do not throw everything into the sea, you will all drown." The ship was full of water. Water! I was so distressed I didn't remember our money was in the backpack. The Mafia took all things in the back [of the boat] and threw them into the sea."

Another refugee shuddered as he told us, "In the inflatable boat, it was a deadly trip—deadly. The

Highlighted in this photo of refugees crammed into a rubber boat are Shakila, a refugee interviewed by TSOS, and her children. Like most land-bound Afghan refugees, Shakila never learned to swim and was terrified for herself and her children during the long, cramped voyage from Turkey to Greece in the flimsy, overloaded boat. She could feel death in the waves that rocked below them and in the vast, open sea that encircled them.

ships, training, and funding to help them intercept refugees at sea and return them to detention centers in Libya. According to an Amnesty International report, detention center guards regularly torture detainees to extort money. They release those who pay and sometimes pass them on to smugglers, who then secure their departure from Libya in boats boat was rubber. That means between us and death was the blink of an eye. We left the shore, and I swear to God I knew I was dead. That's it. We remained on the sea for five hours. Twice the Turks stopped other boats and sent the people in them back, . . . but they didn't stop us. God helped us until we arrived. . . . Praise be to God."

ASYLUM

THE REFUGEE MIGRATION EUROPE IS experiencing is changing the political landscape, and nowhere more so than in Germany, which took in many times more asylum-seekers than any other country. A bureaucratic asylum process is now in place to decide who goes and who stays. The prize is legal status in a safe society full of opportunity for the applicant and his or her children. The penalty, in the worst case, is a one-way ticket back to their homeland and the situation that drove them to pay thousands of dollars, walk thousands of miles and put themselves and their families in grave danger in the first place. . Of the 2015 and 2016 asylum applicants whose fates the government has so far settled, almost half have been rejected.

Key in the asylum process is the personal interview conducted by government employees. Trisha Leimer, TSOS president, has been intimately involved in helping many refugees navigate the asylum bureaucracy. Here she describes the understandable tension felt by refugees while waiting for their interviews:

Gray, stained carpet, brown chairs, gray walls, and a few windows show the rain drizzling in the morning twilight outside. People from Eritrea, Syria, Iran, Afghanistan, or Iraq occupy chairs around the perimeter of the room and try to avoid eye contact, their emotions like a heavy, pressing weight felt by all present. These people have all sold or lost everything, climbed mountains, crossed rivers and seas, waited and worried, then waited longer in anticipation of this day. Today is their asylum hearing, the day when the government hears their stories and decides whether they can stay in Germany or not. They're at the edge of a precipice, straining to see what lies over the edge. My husband and I came to support two displaced friends during this critical interview.

After three hours of quiet whispers and wide-eyed, nervous glances at the open door where the person who controls their destiny could appear at any minute, I pull out a box of lifesavers and jolly ranchers. The reactions are mixed as I walk around the room, stand in front of each nervous person, and offer candy. The sound of wrappers and the sweetness in mouths seems to break the ice. People begin conversations with those next to them, making comments about how badly they slept, how nervous they are, and the drizzle outside.

An hour later, I break out my stash of mandala coloring pages and pass them around along with markers. Most are too nervous to concentrate on coloring designs, but a few welcome the distraction. Sayud, an Iranian man, begins one; two men and a woman from Eritrea work on one together; Muhammad, a young Afghan man with

huge eyes and a round face takes one with a smile; and a young boy from Syria chooses a mandala, works on it for maybe five minutes, then hands it to his older sister, who begins coloring intently.

One by one, names are called, and an electric mix of relief and anxiety impels the designated interviewees to their feet to follow the interpreter out of the room. The interviews are taking three to four hours each; I realize there's no way everyone in the room will be interviewed today. Each time someone returns, they are watched intently by those still waiting for clues as to how things went, clues that might be harbingers of the outcome following their own upcoming reviews.

At 4:30 p.m., when we are told we'll have to come back another day, we feel a collective punch to the gut. The guard urges everyone to go back to their camps, apartments, and group homes and wait for another letter inviting them to return for another judgment day. More anxiety-producing waiting! In the end I am alone in the room with our Iranian friends. We leave feeling dejected, deflated.

Even after the asylum process is complete and the news is good, some refugees still suffer a condition comparable to survivor's guilt. Asad, for instance, found it difficult to be happy even though doors to refuge in France were finally opened to him:

After living for a year in refugee camps, I finally got my asylum interview, and in two months and twenty-two days, I got my answer. When I went to the post office, I was scared. My ears were warm and my feet didn't seem to work. . . . I got the post and read it, but I didn't understand it. I had

Afghan friends with me, and they said, "Asad, you are safe. You are protected!" But I didn't realize it was true until I took it to my social workers, and they read it and hugged me and said, "Congratulations, Asad. You made it!" Somehow it still seemed like I was dreaming.

Even now, when I wake up in the morning, my first thoughts are anxious, but then I remember and tell myself, "No, there is the envelope with your papers. You are safe." During happy times and celebrations, my big brother comes directly into my mind. He couldn't come to Europe; he's still in hiding. And I think, "Are you happy too? Are you fine?" And I think of my wife and son—how to get them to join me here. There is still much to worry about and work for.

Ali stands at the northern rim of Paris where thousands of refugees live destitute on the streets.

HOW YOU CAN HELP

WE ARE AWARE THAT READING STORY AFTER STORY OF TRAUMA, violence, injustice, and despair can be disheartening, but surrounding the dark shadows of human suffering we have encountered unexpected light. The person-to-person, selfless connections that take place between the refugee and the volunteer create unique, bright sparks of hope and optimism. While reading this volume we hope you have felt inspired to connect and become a part of someone's story. No one person, organization or country can possibly relieve all of the human suffering taking place, but these personal connections can and will push back the darkness one spark at a time.

Sharon Eubank, the director of LDS Charities, the humanitarian organization of The Church of Jesus Christ of Latter-day Saints has traveled the world extensively and has a macro view of what is being done across the world. This is her opinion regarding service that accomplishes the most lasting good.

You are the gift. You yourself are the gift. It is not the clothing, the hygiene kits, the school desks, or the wells. It is you.

What would it look like if each of us were our own well-stocked humanitarian organization? Instead of just giving out tangible goods in foreign locations, what if we had the richness of dispensing healing, friendship, respect, peaceful dialogue, sincere interest, protective listening, . . . and conversations with strangers? What if that was what your humanitarian organization did? This kind of humanitarian work can be done by anybody and it can be done at any time. And you don't need warehouses or fundraising or transportation. You can be perfectly responsive to any need that comes to you, wherever you are ("Turning Enemies into Friends," Brigham Young University forum, Jan. 23, 2018.).

HERE'S WHAT YOU CAN DO:

1. SHARE YOUR TALENTS. Thoughtfully consider your own resources and talents and find a way to step across cultural and even geographical borders to give of yourself in simple, meaningful ways. Refugees have many needs: legal support,

financial aid, language and job training, medical assistance, friendship, etc. With today's technology, there are many ways you can fill those needs. Browse through the volunteer pages in this book to refresh your memory on ways to help. You are the gift.

2. **SHARE YOUR STORIES.** Tell us what you are doing to help refugees. Visit our website and click on the 'Contact' button to share your stories and photos; your successes will help give others ideas on how to help.

3. **SHARE THEIR STORIES ONLINE.** Help us spread these stories by sharing them with your family and friends on Facebook, Instagram, and other social media. Visit our website, click on a story and share it to the social media platform of your choice by using the various SHARE icons on the right. You can become their voice by joining the online conversation.

4. **SHARE THEIR STORIES IN PERSON.** Share with your book clubs, special interest groups, women's organizations, workplace service groups, and school classrooms by utilizing our 'Share Their Stories' digital tool kit. On our website hold your mouse over 'Get Involved' in the overhead menu, then click 'Digital Resources' to download free story cards, videos, powerpoint presentations, and other aids.

5. **SHARE YOUR FINANCIAL RESOURCES.** Our team of volunteers relies solely on donated funds to gather and share these stories. Help us continue telling refugee stories by giving TSOS a one-time donation or by signing up for a monthly subscription. Visit our website to donate what you can.

FOR ADDITIONAL IDEAS
ON HOW TO HELP REFUGEES,
VISIT US AT:

tsosrefugees.org

LEARN MORE:
HTTPS://TSOSREFUGEES.ORG/BOOK/LINKS/5

TSOS THEIR STORY IS OUR STORY
giving voice to refugees

Trisha Leimer   Garrett Gibbons   Elizabeth Thayer   Melissa Bradford

Twila Bird   Lydia Defranchi   Noah Read   Matthew Longhurst

Lindsay Silsby   Sarah Wood   Amy Stevenson   Hamed Arian

Christophe Mortier   Kirsti Burton   Nicole Ludwig   Carter Charles

Jordan Pfau   Kathryn Cunningham   Kellie Jolley   Margo Watson

Megan Carson   Phoebe Wood   Tarah Westover   Sarah King

ALL VOLUNTEERS, THEIR STORY IS OUR STORY (TSOS) IS A GROUP of award-winning photographers, filmmakers, painters, writers, and other skilled specialists from Europe and the United States. Our common purpose is to shape international dialogue about refugees by giving them a voice and a platform to tell their stories with the intent to better their situation—and thus ours—worldwide.

PHOTOGRAPHERS & ARTISTS

LINDSAY SILSBY

Lindsay Silsby is a freelance professional photographer based in Dorset, England. With a love of photography since her youth, she has honed her skill and craft in portraiture of families and children. Sharing stories via her lens has always been at the helm of her art. During the refugee crisis, the idea to photograph refugees to better tell their stories came in a dream.

http://piedpiperphoto.com

CHRISTOPHE MORTIER

Distinguished still photographer Christophe Mortier was the recipient of the Portraitist of France award in 2017. He travels to Europe and the Middle East as a keen observer of society. His journalistic photographs have received wide publication and exposure.

www.christophemortier.com

KRISTI BURTON

Kristi Burton is a lifestyle and documentary photographer located in Salt Lake City, Utah. She loves peach pie, dappled light, and reading endless children's books to her adopted daughters.

www.kristiburtonphotography.com

TSOS ARTISTS

ELIZABETH BENSON THAYER

Elizabeth Thayer studied illustration and painting at Brigham Young University, Syracuse University, and UNC Greensboro before settling into motherhood. Always up for adventure, she has lived many places both in the US and abroad; those experiences have both deepened and broadened her perspective and, in turn, the art she creates. She is one of the founding members of TSOS. She recently moved to Utah, where she lives in the shadows of her favorite mountains with her husband and six amazing children.

www.elizabeththayer.com

NATHANEAL READ

Nathaneal Read is an artist and printmaker based in Utah. After feeling a need to put his talents to use in helping others, he began making etchings with TSOS to help refugees tell their stories so we might all see ourselves in their lives.

PHOTOGRAPHY & ARTWORK

CREDITS BY PAGE

LINDSAY SILSBY: front cover, back cover, 2, 6, 8, 10, 14, 19, 21, 22, 26, 29, 35, 40, 42, 45, 49, 53, 59, 63, 67, 69, 73, 75, 76, 79, 81, 85, 96, 99, 103, 105, 106, 107, 112, 115, 121, 122, 125, 126, 127, 128, 129, 151, 157, 158, 162, 168, 177, 179, 180, 185, 186, 193, 195, 196, 199, 205, 207, 208, 217

CHRISTOPHE MORTIER: 32, 36, 46, 50, 52, 54, 60, 80, 91, 104, 105, 130, 133, 135, 139, 137, 145, 147, 148, 152, 153, 170, 183, 188, 202, 218, 227, 230

KRISTI BURTON: 16, 24, 30, 37, 39, 57, 80, 81, 86, 92, 94, 100, 131, 141, 142, 172, 182, 216, 222

ELIZABETH THAYER: 64, 70, 82, 88, 111, 116, 164, 167, 190, 194, 210 (Art); 131, 153, 155 (Photos)

CANDID SHOTS (USED WITH PERMISSION): 12, 24, 25, 53, 81, 104, 119, 130, 131, 152, 182, 183, 219, 224

WIKIMEDIA COMMONS: 220, 223

NATHANEAL READ: 201

ALEX JOHNSON: 161

ABOUT THE PUBLISHER

FAMILIUS IS A GLOBAL TRADE PUBLISHING COMPANY THAT PUBLISHES BOOKS AND other content to help families be happy. We believe that the family is the fundamental unit of society and that happy families are the foundation of a happy life. We recognize that every family looks different, and we passionately believe in helping all families find greater joy. To that end, we publish books for children and adults that invite families to live the Familius Nine Habits of Happy Families: love together, play together, learn together, work together, talk together, heal together, read together, eat together, and laugh together. Founded in 2012, Familius is located in Sanger, California.

FAMILIUS

The most important work you ever do will be within the walls of your own home.